In Home Sales

How To Master One Call Close at The Kitchen Table

By

Shai Ades

IN HOME SALES

Copyright © 2024 by Shai Ades

All rights reserved. No part of this publication may be reproduced, distributed, or transmitted in any form or by any means, including photocopying, recording, or other electronic or mechanical methods, without the prior written permission of the author, except in the case of brief quotations embodied in critical reviews and certain other non-commercial uses permitted by copyright law.

Ordering Information: Quantity sales. Special discounts are available on quantity purchases by corporations, associations, and others. Orders by U.S. trade bookstores and wholesalers.

www.DreamStartersPublishing.com

SHAI ADES

Table of Contents

Dedication 5
Resources 9
Introduction 11
One Call Close Academy 21
Making an Impact 23
Be a Better You 25
Advantages of the One-Call Close 31
Lead Generation 35
Canvassing Pitch 38
Confirmation Script 41
Check Your Attitude 45
Entry 49
Warmup 57
Inspection 63
Six Rules for Inspection 65
Set the Stage 79
Company Story 83
Product Demo 97
Today Page 105
Passing Price with the Work Order 111
Closing 119
Post-Close 141
Taking Care of Your Clients 143
Tips for Success 147
Conclusion 153
Join Our Journey Beyond the Pages 155

IN HOME SALES

Dedication

This book is wholeheartedly dedicated to my loving parents, Daniel and Ines Ades. They embarked on a journey from Montevideo, Uruguay, in November 1989, with a singular dream: to offer my sister, Esther, and me the brightest future possible. They didn't just succeed; they surpassed every expectation. They instilled in us the invaluable virtues of respect and unconditional love. My mother always reminded us that our true wealth lay in the richness of love. She encouraged us to always conduct ourselves as mensches—a Yiddish term for people of integrity and honor. My father imbued us with the belief that anything is achievable. To both of you, from the depths of my heart, thank you for everything. I love you!

To Esther, my heartfelt thanks for your unwavering support and presence in my life. Your friendship and love are treasures I deeply cherish. You have always been an incredible role model for me.

I owe a huge shout-out to Lee Lazar. Our paths have crossed just a few times since my school days, but the lessons he taught me back then have been a guiding light. He was the one who hammered in the urgency of the "now"—a concept that eluded me as a middle schooler fumbling with the idea of studying and thinking I'd magically get it together in high school. Lee made it crystal clear: mastering those skills sooner rather than later wasn't just important; it was crucial. And beyond academics, I've never felt such genuine care and support from a teacher. Lee, your impact is immeasurable. Thank you.

This book is also dedicated to Tyler Ward, who has become both a student and a mentor to me. Initially, I had the privilege of guiding Tyler. But as our journey unfolded, he offered me mentorship in return. His unique insights and fresh perspectives have challenged and reshaped my conventional thinking, contributing significantly to my evolution as a leader, friend, and mentor. His influence has been a pivotal part of my growth, and for that, I am deeply grateful.

This book is lovingly dedicated to my three little princesses: Noa, Ellie, and Abigail. You girls are my entire universe, my driving force, and the keepers of my heart. Each of you has given me invaluable lessons on life and the essence of fatherhood. I eagerly anticipate the journey of watching you grow into incredible young women as we embrace all the adventures that lie ahead of us. My love for you is boundless!

To the cornerstone of my existence, my incredibly amazing wife, Tracy Ades—you are the essence of my world. Without you, I couldn't possibly be the man I am today. Your support and love are beyond words, a profound connection that resonates through every fiber of my being. Every day with you adds another layer to my love, deepening it in ways I never knew possible. You are my rock in tumultuous times, my beacon of encouragement, my challenger, and the lens through which I've discovered new dimensions of life and love.

This book may contain thousands of words, yet none are sufficient to encapsulate the depth of my love and adoration for you. Thank you for being my everything. In the immortal words of Sugarland, "You and me, baby, are stuck like glue." Your presence is my greatest blessing, and I cherish every moment spent with you.

IN HOME SALES

Resources

One Call Close Academy Facebook group: The One Call Close Academy Facebook group is a dynamic online community where sales professionals in the home improvement industry gather to collaborate and share best practices for closing deals on the first visit. Here, members can exchange tips, strategies, and success stories to help each other elevate their sales game and achieve greater success.

OCCA Accelerator Summits: The OCCA Accelerator Summit is an immersive two-day event designed to catapult home improvement sales professionals into new realms of success through proven one-call-close strategies. Attendees engage in intensive workshops and networking opportunities, leaving equipped with the tools, insights, and connections to significantly boost their sales performance and business growth. For more information visit, www.onecallcloseacademy.com

OCCA Vault: The OCCA Vault is an expansive online video library packed with comprehensive training materials designed for sales professionals in the home improvement industry. It offers an array of instructional videos covering everything from mastering the one-call-close technique to advanced sales strategies, empowering users to boost their sales performance and achieve unprecedented success. For more information visit, www.onecallcloseacademy.com

OCCA Sales Tool Box: The OCCA Tool Box: Your Ultimate Sales Strategy Kit for Home Improvement Success, is a concise yet comprehensive eBook designed exclusively for sales professionals in the home improvement and services industry. Packed with practical checklists, this guide covers everything from meticulous inspection forms to essential dos and don'ts for closers, offering valuable insights and tools to streamline your sales process, enhance customer engagement, and secure those crucial one-call closes. Whether you're a seasoned pro or just starting out, this eBook will equip you with the strategies and best practices needed to elevate your sales game to new heights. For your free copy, visit www.onecallcloseacademy.com

@ShaiAdes: My Instagram account is a streaming resource of videos and multimedia, imparting techniques, mindset, and motivation.

Introduction

Have you ever found yourself sitting at a potential client's kitchen table trying to sell your product or service and heard one of these objections?

"We have no money."
"We need to think about it."
"Not now."
"We need to shop around."
"It's too much money."
"I need to talk to my uncle or another family member about it."
"We have other priorities right now."

Whether you are a seasoned sales pro, or new to in-home sales these are the most common objections that homeowners will hit you with. Then we run back to our sales manager and plea with them to help us with our closing. I know that when I was new to the game, this was definitely the case, and now after fifteen years in the home improvement industry I have heard hundreds of sales reps say the same thing. Often we believe these objections and get so frustrated that these tribulations take the wind out of our sails and potentially great reps throw in the towel before they have a chance to taste success.

Not only can these objections be handled and closed, but they can be handled and closed on the first visit without the need to follow up with the potential client. Welcome to my book, where I'll share with you my expertise and experience in the world of sales, specifically focusing on the art of the one-call close. As a seasoned sales professional, I've learned that mastering the one-call close is a game-changer, not just for closing deals but also for skyrocketing your sales numbers and achieving greater success in your career.

The one-call close is a powerful selling technique that involves closing a client on the very first visit, without the need for follow-up calls or additional visits. It's not an easy technique to master, but it's highly effective in various industries, including real estate, insurance, home improvements, pest control, and direct sales. My knowledge and expertise are in the home improvement space.

To achieve success in the one-call close, you need to have a strategic approach. That approach should involve building trust and rapport with the customer, identifying their needs and desires, and being able to communicate effectively and persuasively. You need to have a strong sales pitch that highlights your company, along with your product or service, while addressing any objections or concerns the customer may have. Your goal is to convince the customer to act and make that purchase.

As someone who has found success with this method, I can attest that the one-call close is beneficial to both the client and the salesperson. It saves everyone's time by eliminating the need for multiple follow-up visits. It also reduces the salesperson's travel time, ensuring that they and the company can focus on seeing new clients and increasing their sales numbers, leading to significant rewards.

In the world of sales, practice doesn't just make perfect—it makes profits. One-call close sales are the ultimate training ground for any sales rep eager to sharpen their skills. It's all about the frequency of opportunities, or as we like to call it, getting multiple "at-bats" every day.

In industries like software sales, the sales cycle can be a marathon, often stretching over six months. While every sale is a chance to learn and improve, these extended cycles mean it can take a long time to refine your approach and even longer to see the results of those refinements.

Contrast that with the one-call close environment. Here, the sales cycle is condensed into a couple of hours. Every day presents multiple opportunities to pitch, negotiate, and close. With each "at-bat," you're not just swinging for the fences; you're adjusting your stance, perfecting your swing, and learning how to hit different pitches. The rapid feedback loop of one-call close sales allows you to quickly learn what works, what doesn't, and how to change strategies on the fly. The lessons stick because they're repeated often; and success comes faster because you're constantly applying and evolving your tactics.

Embrace the pace of one-call close sales. Let the intensity forge your skills in the fire of real-world practice. If you can master the quick pitch and close of this environment, you'll be well on your way to becoming a seasoned sales professional who can thrive in any selling situation.

In this book, I'll guide you through the process of mastering the art of the one-call close. You'll learn the key techniques and strategies that will help you achieve success with this type of sale. Whether you're a seasoned salesperson or new to the industry, this book will equip you with the tools you need to close more deals and achieve greater success in your career.

By the end of this book, you'll have a deep understanding of the one-call close technique and how to use it to your advantage. You'll be able to build trust and rapport with your customers, address objections and concerns, and persuade them to make a purchase. So, get ready to discover the super-rewarding world of the one-call close and take your sales career to the next level.

Lessons Learned

I have been in the one-call close home improvement space for 15 years. My entire life I have had a passion for sales, and as a young kid I always imagined myself wearing nice suits and talking business. I had no idea what it meant or where I would end up, but I knew I had a gift for gab and an extroverted personality that needed to rub elbows with people.

My first job after college, besides working at a beach sports camp, was waiting tables and selling weed, making roughly 2,000 to 2,500 dollars a month. I went to my first sales interview in a 1969 Volkswagen bus. I got the job, but after eight months of banging out cold calls for a vulnerability management company, I was fired. In that short-lived opportunity, I was making 200 calls a day while getting Nerf darts launched at my face. When that wasn't happening, I was running across the street to Coffee Bean to get my manager's coffee. In retrospect, getting fired was hardly surprising—I had only made one sale, and my manager had closed it for me.

After smoking my brains out to cope with being fired, I decided to start interviewing for jobs again. Although I only made one sale in those eight months, I learned some valuable life skills that allowed me to soar very quickly once I got into the one-call close home improvement space. I learned to say my name with pride and to speak up. Most importantly, I learned that it is not necessary to reinvent the wheel—just learn from those at the top. Unfortunately, I did not learn these lessons quickly enough at that first sales job, but once I put them into action, they catapulted my success.

My introduction to the one-call close business was during my week-long stint of job interviews, involving multiple interviews a day. It was my second or third interview on a Tuesday, and this woman was explaining home improvement sales on commission only. The idea was appealing. There was potential, but also enormous risk. I was already broke. How could I even think about taking a commission-only job? What if I didn't sell anything? What if I failed? So, I moved on and continued to interview, but all I could think about was this home improvement opportunity. Eventually, I decided to go back for a second interview.

One thing I did when I went back in was to look over the sales board. What was the top guy doing? What was the bottom guy doing? The commission structure was attractive. The fact that I would be out in the field all day and not connected to a phone was also appealing.

Then there was the concept of closing people the same day you met them. The software world had more of a six-to-twelve-month sales process. Can you imagine pretending to like someone and shmoozing them for six to twelve months only to have them let you down in the end and go with one of your competitors?

While you may not win every deal in the one-call close world, after three hours and several no's, you cut your losses and move on to the next one. No strings attached, you dust yourself off, analyze what you think you did well and what you can improve on, and then it is on to the next potential customer.

So, I jumped in headfirst and gave it a shot. It started with a week-long training class, where I studied my brains out. This meant waking up early and writing out the scripts; then staying up late and studying the scripts. I would pitch my girlfriend, Tracy (now my wife). I would pitch an empty couch. I needed to make this work.

Two weeks into the job, I sold an exterior paint and stucco lead for $17,323 to a sweet lady in Long Beach, California. Boom! I could do this! Then, in less than 24 hours, the job cancelled. Fuck! My manager tried to save the deal, but that one couldn't be saved. What could we do? A group of men from her church told her they would paint her house for free.

After that, it took me 30 days to get my next close. A lot of the veteran reps were selling daily, and there was just something I couldn't figure out. The problem was I believed all the homeowner's objections. I believed them and justified them to myself. My frustration was growing while my savings account was shrinking. I was away from home six days a week from 8 a.m. until as late as 10 p.m. My money was going toward gas, food, coffee, and weed; and I had nothing to show for my efforts.

In those first 30 days, I almost quit ten separate times. Tracy was my rock and supported me the entire time. Every time I got discouraged, she would tell me to keep going. Finally, on day 31, I got a real sale! Then I got another on day 32, and two more on days 33 and 35! Finally, something had clicked, and I was off to the races. Ninety days later, I was promoted to assistant manager; and a year later, sales manager. Not long after that I became Director of Sales. My Audi Q7 was paid for. I bought a house, went on vacations, and got an amazing engagement ring.

In my first few years in management, I trained a couple dozen sales reps, taking people with the same financial background as me when I started and teaching them, very quickly, how to make a six-figure income. However, the owner of the business treated my team poorly, leading them to leave just as they became successful. It was the definition of insanity: I would pour my heart and soul into training these men, only for them to seek greener pastures where their commissions weren't cut, and they were treated with respect. After a few years of being trapped on this hamster wheel, it was time for me to move on as well. I couldn't stand grooming these men to be champions, only to lose them to competitors. As I outgrew my old boss, I knew it was time to find a company where my reps were treated better and my efforts were truly valued.

    Since leaving, I have worked for a few different companies and started a few as well. I have taken companies from less than $300,000 a month to $800,000 a month, and others from $0 to $23 million, in less than a year. I have taken businesses that started with two sales reps and one location, and grown them to have a sales team of 34 with three locations.

IN HOME SALES

Chapter 1

One Call Close Academy

Unbeknownst to me, my business partner was not handling the office properly, and after multiple problems with homeowners and subcontractors, the business license was revoked. After the unfortunate dissolution of my partnership and the subsequent loss of the business license due to my ex-partner's mismanagement, I found myself at a crossroads. It was a moment filled with uncertainty yet brimming with potential. My experiences, both triumphant and challenging, had equipped me with an unparalleled depth of knowledge in the sales and home improvement arena. Determined to turn this setback into an opportunity, I decided to channel my skills and talents into a new venture—One Call Close Academy.

IN HOME SALES

One Call Close Academy was born out of a desire to transform the home improvement and home service industry by sharing the lessons I've learned and the strategies I've developed over the years, both in the field and in the office. My mission was clear: to elevate businesses from merely surviving to thriving by mastering the art of the one-call close. This consulting company is dedicated to helping business owners and sales reps achieve success by leveraging my expertise and turning challenges into triumphs.

Tidal Remodeling, based in Carlsbad, California, became a cornerstone case-study for One Call Close Academy. Beginning our journey together in June 2023, we set ambitious targets. In its first year, Tidal achieved an impressive six million dollars in revenue in seven months, a testament to the power of refined sales strategies and a well-trained, respected sales force. Today, our sights are set far higher. For 2024, we are targeting an audacious goal of 50 million dollars in revenue. It's a goal that, to some, may seem out of reach. But with the right mindset, training, and sales processes in place, I have every confidence that Tidal Remodeling will not only meet but exceed this target.

Chapter 2

Making an Impact

This consulting journey isn't just about numbers; it's about impact. It's about changing the narrative around sales in the home improvement industry, and proving that respect, integrity, and empowerment are not just ideals but actionable principles that drive success. My past experiences, especially the challenges, have shaped me into the consultant I am today: focused, driven, and unwaveringly committed to the success of my clients.

As One Call Close Academy continues to grow, I aim to replicate the success we've seen with Tidal Remodeling across the industry, transforming the way home improvement businesses operate and compete. Through this work, I not only find redemption for the trials of my past, but I am also able to pave the way for a new generation of businesses built

IN HOME SALES

on foundations of respect, excellence, and, most importantly, extraordinary results.

Chapter 3

Be a Better You

    I love the industry, but more than anything I am passionate about taking ordinary individuals and making them extraordinary. Watching individuals who never made more than $20,000 in their life, making close to $150,000 12 months into the business is inspiring. These are often people who didn't own any car, who then end up buying their dream car. I have watched reps move out of their parent's home, and into their new rented apartment, and then from their rented apartment into their first home. I have watched salespeople take what I have taught them and create lifelong careers. Some have even started their own companies and are extremely successful. It's great to get a random text message now and then from someone thanking me for where they are in life. Those messages fuel my soul and warm my heart more than any paycheck I have ever received.

Many of my students have been able to level up because learning to be a one-call closer involves more than just learning to close a homeowner. It involves learning how to level up as a person as well. It involves learning how to create short-term, mid-term, and long-term goals; dreaming BIG and then reverse engineering life to get there. To do incredible work you have to look, feel, and act incredible. How you talk to yourself matters. What you think about matters.

As the great Anthony Robbins has said time and time again, "Energy flows where attention goes. To get what you want in life, you need a clear goal that has purpose and meaning behind it. Once this is in place, you can focus your energy on the goal and become obsessive about it."

Are you merely interested in your goals or are you committed to them? Do you write them down or do you just think about them? If you just think about them, they are not real, you are not obsessed. It is only when you write down your goals that you have enough clarity about them, enabling you to take concrete steps toward making them reality. Michael Hyatt, author of "Your Best Year Ever," identifies five reasons why writing down your goals is so important. "First, it forces you to clarify what you want...second, writing down your goals helps you overcome resistance...third, it motivates you to take action…fourth, it filters other opportunities… and fifth, it enables you to see and celebrate your progress." Some days will be harder than others, and without a clear "why" to motivate you through challenging times, the tough days will be tougher. You cannot learn to be a better closer without learning to be a better person.

Tom Hopkins will tell you "Selling is the highest-paid hard work—and the lowest-paid easy work." The decision to work hard or easy is all yours.

Along with writing down your goals, you should have a solid morning routine. How do you start your day? How do you look at this incredible opportunity that you have been given? Do you roll out of bed and run to your first appointment, or do you have a morning routine prior to that first appointment?

One of the most important things I impart to my staff and students is the importance of a morning routine.

Hal Elrod, author of "The Miracle Morning," says. "How you wake up each day and your morning routine (or lack thereof) dramatically affects your level of success in every single area of your life. Focused, productive, successful mornings generate focused, productive, successful days—which inevitably create a successful life—in the same way that unfocused, unproductive, and mediocre mornings generate unfocused, unproductive, and mediocre days, and ultimately a mediocre quality of life."

Starting the day with a morning routine, having a structured start to the day, can help sales reps prepare for the challenges and opportunities ahead. By starting each day with activities such as exercise, meditation, or reading, sales reps can prime their minds and bodies for a productive day. This can help increase focus, energy, and motivation, allowing them to better engage with potential customers and close deals.

Moreover, having a morning routine can help sales reps establish a sense of control and discipline, which can carry over into their work. By taking charge of their mornings, sales reps can develop the confidence and mental fortitude needed to tackle challenging sales situations, among other tough situations.

On the other hand, a negative or stressed mental state can hinder a sales rep's performance. Sales can be a high-pressure and demanding job, and if a sales rep is feeling overwhelmed or anxious, they may struggle to connect with potential customers or communicate effectively. A rep who is running behind for appointments or feeling anxious because of the lack of a morning routine is setting himself up for complete failure. The stress and fatigue that one puts on themselves can result in missed opportunities and lost sales.

There is nothing better than seeing happy individuals better themselves through healthy habits, such as a consistent morning routine and a positive mental state. By establishing healthy habits and cultivating a strong mindset, sales reps can increase their productivity, focus, and resilience, and ultimately achieve greater success in their sales efforts. This can all be summed up by a quote from Jim Rohn: "Your level of success, will rarely exceed your level of personal development, because success is something you attract by the person you become."

IN HOME SALES

Chapter 4

Advantages of the One-Call Close

The one-call close technique is important for salespeople because it can lead to increased sales volume, reduced costs associated with follow-up visits or calls, improved customer satisfaction, and more efficient use of time for the salesperson. Instead of wasting hours chasing potential clients through follow-up appointments, sales reps can either celebrate their win or cut their losses and move on to the next prospect. How much time and energy have sales reps lost in the past chasing the same deal that never comes to fruition? How many new opportunities are lost? What does this do to a representative's self-esteem?

IN HOME SALES

The one-call close sale process is unlike any other. It goes against what most people are taught and against most people's instincts. Conventional wisdom says that very few people would ever buy a large ticket item on a salesperson's first visit and without any further research. Yet the one-call close industry has been around for ages and will continue to be around forever.

To understand one-call closing, one must understand that it is an EMOTIONAL SALE SUPPORTED BY LOGIC. There have been countless successful closes which began with homeowners adamantly saying they would not sign anything on their first visit or that they would need to get three estimates before they move forward with anything. The three-estimate rule is the responsible thing to do, and when most sales reps hear this, they look for any reason to leave and get a fresh "interested" lead. They think that pitching these people would be a waste of their time. They could not be more wrong. This is still an opportunity to close, and once you do, the customer will never get the other bids they thought they would.

With the one-call close, salespeople can save time by eliminating the need for multiple follow-up visits or calls, allowing them to see more clients and increase their sales numbers. How many times have you heard people say that sales is a numbers game? The key factor is that they have to be new numbers not just recycling the same ones over and over again. This technique can also help build trust and rapport with customers, as it is designed to project knowledge and confidence from the salesperson.

The one-call close technique can also lead to improved customer satisfaction, as customers appreciate the convenience of being able to make a purchase or sign a contract on the first visit, usually in their own home. This not only simplifies their decision-making process, preventing decision fatigue, but also encourages taking immediate action on matters they might otherwise delay until it's too late, due to life's inevitable distractions. By facilitating a decision in one visit, we help ensure that important decisions get made promptly, which can prevent future complications for the client. This approach can lead to increased referrals and repeat business, as satisfied customers appreciate the streamlined, purposeful experience.

Overall, mastering the one-call close technique can be highly beneficial for salespeople who are looking to maximize their results and achieve greater success in their careers. Plus, for the salesperson, it allows you to be yourself and let your personality shine. It can be a real confidence booster. There is no glass ceiling on earning potential. Just about every year that I have done this I have had a representative break the previous year's record.

There are challenges to overcome, but those can easily become beneficial as well. Using this method prevents you from getting bored and settling for mediocrity. You get to be challenged and have fun. Yes, work can be fun! To be an expert in this field requires skill, strategy, and effective communication, but once you master those things the rewards can be significant. While the monetary reward is incredible, the ego boost and self-confidence gained from being a one-call closer is outstanding—especially if you are doing this at a high level.

There is no other sales job that holds a candle to a one-call closer career. We have all heard the phrase "No man walks on the lot unless he wants to buy." In most sales jobs you wait for the customer to walk on the lot. If you work at Best Buy, people come in to buy electronics. If you sell cars, people come to the dealership to buy them. Even if you sell real estate, the potential buyer calls you to show them the property. One-call closing is different, and to do well, you must have a skill that most other salespeople lack. If you are thriving in this industry you are likely in the top one percent of salespeople.

Chapter 5

Lead Generation

There are various types of lead sources in the one-call close business. A majority of the leads myself and my staff run are door-to-door canvassed leads. The appointments are usually scheduled 24 hours or less from first contact and, in my opinion, are the hottest leads out there. If they are set further out than 24 hours, you at least want to make sure they are not more than 72 hours. People have busy lives and will forget about the appointment if the lead is not reconfirmed in that time period.

The thing to understand about door-to-door canvassed leads is that these are not interested buyers. They were not out looking for your product or service. They were closed by the canvasser pointing out some damage, creating a need, and connecting emotionally with the homeowner. The fact that they are standing right there, face-to-face with the homeowner adds a personal touch that can help build trust and credibility. Plus, people are generally nicer in person than they are over the phone.

Another advantage of door-to-door lead generation is that appointment setters can create immediate need and urgency. Unlike telemarketing and other forms of marketing, the appointment setter is looking directly at the damage. This allows them to tailor their pitch precisely to the homeowner's situation. This personalized approach can help overcome objections and lead to a higher likelihood of booking an appointment.

Finally, door-to-door leads can also be less competitive than other forms of lead generation. These homeowners are not actively seeking home improvement services. Homeowners may be more likely to entertain a sales pitch when there are no other options readily available.

The most critical task for generating door-to-door appointments is to create a NEED for the homeowner. Often the need is not created by simply pointing out damage, but by pointing out the consequences of not taking care of the damage.

It is also imperative to get a homeowner to think about their current situation, and this is most effectively done by asking good, qualifying questions. For example, if I was setting up an exterior paint lead, I would ask the homeowner the following questions:

- *"How long have you owned the home?" (I want to make sure I am talking to the owner.)*
- *"When was the last time you painted?"*
- *"Who did it?"*
- *"Is this the worst of the damage or are there other areas of concern?"*
- *"I know you're not doing this anytime soon, but when you do, will you change the color?"*
- *"When was the last time you had a termite inspection?"*

What I am doing by asking all these questions is: First, keeping their mind busy answering my questions so they can't think of objections; and second, getting them to think about their situation and creating that critical need.

IN HOME SALES

Canvassing Pitch

Intro

Good morning/good afternoon. Beautiful home. The reason I stopped by is I noticed ... (identify the specific damage).

Quick question, how long have you owned this beautiful home?

Educate

Did you know that _____ is going to allow moisture into the home that can lead to dry rot, termites, and toxic mold? Eventually, you're going to get your roof repaired, right? (Create need/urgency and ask qualifying questions.)

- Is your roof leaking?
- When was the last time you popped your head in the attic?
- Does anyone in the home have any respiratory issues?
- I know you're not doing this now, but when you do, are you thinking about changing the colors?

Close

Here is what I'm going to do. My guys are in the area. I'm going to put you at the top of my list for a free inspection tomorrow. What time works best for you and your spouse, MORNING or AFTERNOON? Two or six?

Get Info

Excuse me, my name is _____. And you are? And how do I spell your last name? And how do I spell your spouse's name?
And your address is 123 _____ Street? And this is 92107? Just in case we are running a little late—we value your time—the best number to get a hold of you is 619 or 760?

Separate The Spouse

Now tomorrow at ___ is a good time for you? You won't be on work calls or going to the gym? And your spouse, she won't be picking up the kids or working away from home?

Set The Stage

Now tomorrow at ___ my guy will come out and do a full inspection for you. He'll take measurements and pictures.

Then he will sit down with you, show you a copy of our license, bond, insurance—all our credentials—then show you some styles and options to choose from. You'll get an exact price in writing for if and when you're ready. FAIR ENOUGH?

Confirmation

In the next five to ten minutes, my office is going to give you a call to confirm tomorrow's appointment. If you do not answer the call, there will be no inspection and they will send me back. Have a great day!

     Other forms of lead generation include telemarking, social media, home shows, events, referrals, and call-ins. Regardless of how the lead was generated, they can all be closed using the methods in this book. Recognizing the nature of each lead is crucial, discerning whether it's driven by emotion or logic. Emotional leads are those that are spontaneous: door-to-door, telemarketing, social media, and events. The prospect did not see you coming. It was a random interaction in which we were able to spike their curiosity, create a need, and book an appointment. The other lead sources, such as home shows, referrals, and some types of social media, are logical lead sources. The prospect was out searching for your service.

Some of these lead sources can also fall under both categories. Social media leads, for example, come through a pop-up ad (emotional) or a web search (logical). Referrals and self-generated appointments can also fall under both categories depending on how the initial contact was made: emotional if you knocked on a neighbor's door, logical if the neighbor came and talked to you while you were on the job site.

Once a lead is generated, we always confirm the appointment over the phone through our confirmation department. This means confirming all the information we have is correct: name, address, date, time, and product; and that ALL the homeowners will be there. Since we are a one-call close shop, we always want to increase our odds of pitching all the decision-makers at once.

Confirmation Script

Confirmer: Hi. Is this John? My name is Mark with XYZ calling to confirm your roof inspection appointment. How was my guy _____ just now, nice and polite?

Homeowner: Yes, he was.

IN HOME SALES

Confirmer: Excellent. John can you spell your last name for me real quick?

Homeowner: S-M-I-T-H

Confirmer: Great. Thank you. And your spouse's name, please?

Homeowner: M-A-R-Y

Confirmer: Perfect. I have your address as 100 Park Plaza, San Diego 92101. Is that correct?

Homeowner: Yes.

Confirmer (IF LEAD IS A ROOF): Now John, tell me a little about the roof. Is it currently leaking? No? Great to hear. Do you know the last time it was replaced? Ok, not a problem. I know you're not going to do it now, but when you do, do you have a color in mind you'd like to see?

Confirmer (IF LEAD IS **PAINT**): Now John, tell me a little about the exterior. Is it stucco or siding? Do you know the last time it was painted? OK. What are the areas concerning you the most? No problem. And John, I know you are not going to get it painted right now, but when you do, do you have any colors in mind?

Separate The Spouse

Confirmer: Great, and as for tomorrow, is 10 a.m. the best time for you? You're not going to the gym or working from home?

Homeowner: No, that works.

Confirmer: Excellent. And how about Mary; 10 a.m. works for her as well? No yoga class or girls' trips planned?

Homeowner: Yes, that works for her as well.

Set The Stage

Confirmer: Amazing. So when my guy gets there tomorrow, he will do a thorough corner-to-corner inspection, share with you our licensing & credentials, show you some styles and options to choose from, and give you an exact price in writing for if and when you're ready. Fair enough?

An estimate takes approximately one hour plus the time for questions you may have, sound good?

IN HOME SALES

Confirmer: (IF YES) Awesome. Once again, thank you so much for your time, and we are looking forward to meeting with you tomorrow. Enjoy the rest of your day.

Confirmer: (IF NO) No problem. I'll have my guy give you the Reader's Digest version. Fair enough?

Amazing. Once again, thank you so much for your time, and we are looking forward to meeting with you tomorrow. Enjoy the rest of your day.

After the lead is fully confirmed it is time to get a sales representative out to the home as quickly as possible. As mentioned before, we typically schedule our appointments for the very next day. There are even circumstances where we book them for the same day the canvasser knocked on the door, especially if that is the only time in the near future that the homeowner will be available.

Chapter 6

Check Your Attitude

Once you or your representative is at the appointment you must not prejudge the homeowners or their situation. Try to avoid or overcome any preconceived notions you have about whether or not the prospect will buy. Common ones include:

- The house is a mess; they'll never buy.
- They look like they don't have money; they'll never buy.
- They are of a certain race or ethnicity, and I never sell these.

IN HOME SALES

Preconceived beliefs like these soon become self-fulfilling prophecies. If you believe you can't, you won't. You should be aware of that proverbial little guy on your shoulder who's always telling you, "They'll never buy." Just make sure you don't listen to him!

Remember, nothing ever happens unless a presentation is made. If you fail to present because of the reasons above or similar ones, you are committing economic suicide. If they own the home and they are present, this is a GOOD LEAD. This is one of the most difficult aspects to teach new sales reps. They say these people live in a shitty neighborhood and will never buy, or they don't do well with people of a particular race, or they don't do well with single men or single ladies. These are negative thoughts that should never be in your head.

To thrive in this industry, you must believe that you can close anyone, anywhere, anytime! The late Zig Ziglar once said, "It's your attitude, not your aptitude that will determine your altitude." Meaning, to be successful in any area of life you need to have the right attitude to approach any task or job.

Also, to improve in or learn a new job you must be willing to put in the reps and check your ego at the door. As Albert Einstein once said, "When you stop learning you start dying." All great salespeople are like great athletes in the sense that they do the basics very well and repeat them often.

The faster you check your ego and prepare yourself to grind, the faster you will have the life you desire.

The fastest way to learn something is by being interested in it. The more psyched and excited you are about a subject, the faster you will retain the information. Once you have learned the information, you have to repeat it over and over again. We are all familiar with the quote, "Repetition is the mother of learning." The faster you engrave these words and concepts into you, the faster they become a part of you. Just like muscles get stronger with repeated use, your skills improve with consistent practice. It's proven that people who go to the gym and suddenly stop begin to regress by day three. Similarly, if we stop using the information we've learned, we regress.

Continuous learning and practice are crucial. Like athletes, we need to revisit the basics every couple of weeks. Ignoring what got us to where we are and thinking we're now super sales reps can lead to slipping back to a place we don't want to be. Even as we grow and improve, we must not lose sight of the fundamentals that built our foundation.

Now that we have our mind right, let's move on to the entry. Although it sounds so simple, to enter the home, this is one of the steps I spend the most time teaching to a new training class. Simply stated: if you cannot get into the home, none of the other steps matter.

IN HOME SALES

Steps to a one-call close sale:

1. Entry - Throw away the sale.
2. Warm-up - Establish rapport and qualify the homeowner.
3. Inspection - Use the doctor's approach.
4. Set the Stage - Give the homeowner expectations for the day and change the tone from consultation to sales call.
5. Company Story - Sell your company. Differentiate yourself from your competitors and industry standards.
6. Product Demonstration - Educate them on options and why yours is the best one.
7. Today Page - Trial closes and narrow it down to money.
8. Pass price with the work order.
9. Close
10. Post Close

Chapter 7

Entry

No one likes to be sold, but everyone likes to buy. We all know this and have heard this phrase before. But if people don't like to be sold how does this work? We have to throw away the sale. The homeowner cannot know that you are a shark.

Times have changed. Back in the day, people took pride in being a salesperson. It was associated with men wearing good-looking suits and driving Cadillacs. But society has changed, and no one likes salespeople these days. The largest companies in the world now advertise their sales positions as business development representatives or account managers. Salespeople at Apple are called specialists and business experts. At Lululemon they call them educators. At

IN HOME SALES

Ulta they are called Beauty Advisors. They are all just salespeople.

Because the one-call close business usually involves showing up at a potential customer's door, this idea of "throwing away the sale" is even more important. In today's society, people are more guarded than ever before. People live petrified, the TV news is all bad, the radio news is worse, and homeowners are more skeptical than ever. Because of this, the most difficult part of the sale could simply be getting yourself inside the door.

Most of the leads that I ran were generated by door-to-door canvassers, setting up "free inspections," with homeowners for either a roof, exterior paint, windows, or turf and pavers. Most of the time, these were not interested prospects who were thinking about doing something to their home. These were people who had their door knocked on in the last 24 hours and who were convinced by a very good appointment setter to get a free inspection for one of our products.

Often when I would get to the door for my appointment I was greeted with objections or excuses on why the homeowners could not sit down with me that day:

- *"We called to cancel."*
- *"We don't want to waste your time because we are not doing anything."*

- *"We have no money."*
- *"I am going to do the work myself,"* or *"We already have a guy."*
- *"We're not interested."*
- *"I don't know why my spouse made the appointment."*

Some of my biggest sales started with the most resistance at the door. You have two choices when confronted with these, believe their bullshit and drive off to Starbucks to waste more time and money, or stay in the pocket and get through the door. Obviously, I am a big believer in the second option. I have trained countless sales reps to not believe the resistance at the door and to continue working the system. Often the bigger the homeowners bark at the beginning, the easier the close is at the end if you manage to get in to pitch. They barked so much at the beginning that they had no energy left at the end.

We also need to step back for a minute and remember that this is a human-to-human connection, and we are pretty funny humans. Think about yourself entering your favorite department store to buy something.

You walk in, start browsing around, and within minutes a sales associate comes up and asks, "May I help you?"

What do you and the rest of us all say back? "No thank you. Just looking."

IN HOME SALES

It's human nature to resist or to protect ourselves in this situation, even when we are shopping for something and likely to make a purchase.

So, why do homeowners give you resistance when they make an appointment with your company? Oftentimes, it's fear of buying. They know that if they let you in, they are going to spend money. So, it is their last-ditch effort to keep themselves from buying something. Sometimes they don't let you in because they are not in the same state of mind they were in yesterday, or even earlier that day when the door-to-door guy came by. Life happens, and the marketer just happened to get a better two minutes of these people's lives. A lot can change in a few minutes, hours, or days since the appointment was set.

But there we are at the door. Our number one goal is to get inside the house. We just want to cross that threshold and start to build rapport with our client. People will always treat you better inside their home than outside. But, if you act like a sleazy sales rep, no one will invite you in to get your sales process started.

One of the most effective techniques I teach for getting in the door is called Aikido. You might be familiar with Aikido as a form of martial arts. Originating in Japan in the 1920s, Aikido was created by Morihei Ueshiba. This martial art emphasizes using an opponent's energy and movements to defend oneself and neutralize attacks. Practitioners learn to blend with the attacker's motion, redirecting the force rather than opposing it head-on. The techniques involve joint locks, throws, and strikes, minimizing harm to both parties.

In sales, the principles of Aikido can be incredibly powerful. The key lies in listening, empathy, and understanding—essential skills for any successful salesperson. By carefully listening to a prospect's needs and concerns, you can tailor your approach to better meet those needs, building trust and rapport in the process.

Aikido also teaches non-resistance. In sales, this translates to remaining open-minded and flexible in your approach. Instead of pushing for a sale, an Aikido-influenced salesperson seeks to understand the prospect's perspective and find a mutually beneficial solution. This technique fosters a positive interaction and increases the likelihood of closing the sale by addressing the prospect's true needs.

If someone told me they called to cancel, I would immediately respond, "Sure no problem, we can reschedule for a better time, what happened here?" What I am doing is giving empathy, making them feel heard, and then redirecting the conversation. Generally, humans only use 10% of their brain, so the only thing they will respond to is the last thing I said: "What happened here?" They will then answer my question and I will move on. Their objection (lie) is forgotten, and I can keep moving forward with my presentation.

IN HOME SALES

Another option for the "I called to cancel" objection is to flip the script on the homeowner. I would say, "Why did you make the appointment anyway? Your home is gorgeous." They would then proceed to tell me everything that was wrong with the house. Now they are telling me their problems, and that will naturally lead into my presentation.

If someone told me, "You're wasting your time, we have no money," again I would empathize.

"Sure, no problem," I'd reply, and then move on. "I'm just here for a look and a price, we won't need any money today." I am disarming the homeowner, alleviating their scared mindset, and demonstrating an even playing field. Then I would move forward with my presentation.

Getting into the house is remarkably simple. You must speak confidently and have the proper body language. I simply introduce myself, wipe my feet on the door mat, regardless of whether they have one or not, and ask to come in: "Hi Barbara, my name is Shai Ades with XYZ company. We have a two o'clock appointment. May I come in?" My hand is extended to shake their hand, while at the same time I am wiping my feet. The wiping of my feet is a universal sign that I am coming in. Once I have made it through the threshold, I am on to step number two, which is my warmup.

I know this is an unorthodox style of selling, but if you don't sell away from selling, the homeowners will not listen to your presentation. We cannot sell home improvements while our feet are still on the doormat.

A sales rep needs to understand what to expect when they arrive at an appointment. It is an appointment, not an "interested" prospect. The first and most important job of a sales rep is to get inside the home and start the sales process. A definition of a "good appointment" is that all buying parties are present.

Since you are giving them information on a home improvement product, they will assume you want to measure or inspect the house first. But you must get inside the house. If you let them have control here, your chances of selling are greatly reduced. Don't give up. Some of the largest sales are made when they say, "Just measure and leave the estimate in the mailbox." Keep knocking and get to the couch.

The "entry" is used to break the ice between you and the homeowner, but it is not merely small talk. It is not our goal to make friends with the prospect. From the moment you park your car in front of the house, the sales stopwatch is running. Every choice you make must be focused on achieving the sale—that is your goal at entry.

Unfortunately, because homeowners are human you may not be able to pitch every single lead. Sometimes you will be faced with a disgruntled homeowner or someone who is just having a difficult day. Nevertheless, you must find a way to win. If you don't win, you lose. And if you lose, you'll pay

IN HOME SALES

the price of feeling like a loser on your next appointment. There are three ways to win:

1. You obviously win when you make a sale.
2. You win when you sell your way in to make a presentation.
3. You win when you reset an appointment due to a condition when you successfully resell the appointment.

You can (and must) think of yourself as winning when you know you did everything humanly possible to close the sale, but simply could not close it at this time.

Chapter 8

Warmup

Nobody buys from people they don't like. It's one of the most basic principles. Have you ever walked out of a store or not bought something simply because you didn't like the sales associate helping you? I know I have, and my wife, who is very service-oriented, has many times. So, how do we get someone to like us?

It starts with your appearance. There is never a second chance to make a first impression. So, your approach is crucial. Your entry must be smooth and nonthreatening, or you will never even have the chance to warm up with your customer.

Let's assume you make it through the threshold and you're sitting on their couch. Who are you speaking with? Since our goal is to walk out of the home with a sale today, we want to ensure that we are talking to all the homeowners at the same time. If you talk to only the husband or only the wife, the objections will be very predictable. "Everything sounds great, but I need to speak to my spouse." So, we must be presenting to both homeowners.

      Sometimes reps feel that they can get away with just talking to the husband because construction is "man's business." But in many families the wife controls the finances, and whether or not she knows anything about roofing or painting, she knows what 10k, 20k, 30k, or more looks like leaving the family bank account. On the other hand, if you only speak with the wife, the husband will suggest shopping around and getting a cheaper bid simply because he was not there to receive the information. Remember this is an emotional sale supported by logic. Everyone who will be making the decision needs to go through the ark of emotion that we create with our presentation.

      Next, it is imperative to gather as much information as you can. You have not entered the "negotiation" part yet, and their defenses are not yet in place. You should notice how they live and what is happening. Are they relaxed or rushed? Is dinner on the stove? Are they both present and seemingly interested? It is here that you start to build rapport and ask your qualifying questions, which will later lead to the inspection part of the demonstration.

Most reps say building rapport is easy. People like me can just wing it, right? WRONG. This is a major hazard for many sales reps who do not take their profession seriously. They believe they have a likable personality and can talk to anyone, so they just plow ahead and ask the homeowners a bunch of questions about themselves. Not only does this not always work, but you may also agitate your potential buyer. You must be prepared. You must be professional.

I recommend having a warm-up sheet like the ones below. Not only does it give you a guide to follow, but it also ensures you look professional. You are not interrogating the homeowner with questions; you are doing your job. The goal is not to be merely liked by the homeowner but to be perceived as the trusted authority. It's not a popularity contest. They want to know that you can get the job done professionally and achieve the best results for them.

IN HOME SALES

Home Inspection Form - Roof

Customer : ....

Date : ....

Roof

How long have you owned the home?

How old is your roof?

How many Layers Currently?

Last time re-roofed and why?

Water intrusion in Attic?

Interested in color Change? Y/N What Color?

When was your last termite inspection?

Do you have any concerns with your roof?

Attic

When was the last time you had an attic inspection?

Do you have any insulation? If so, how much?

Gutters

Do you have a gutter system?

When is the last time you had your gutter system checked?

Solar

Any Solar Panels on the Roof? Y/N

Interested In Solar? Y/N

Average monthly bill?

SHAI ADES

Home Inspection Form - Exterior Paint

Customer: ....

Date : ....

General

How long have you owned the home?

- When was the last time you painted?
- Do you want to change the color or keep it the same?
- What do you like most about your home's exterior? What do you dislike the most?

Stucco

- Do you have any damaged stucco on the house? If so, where?
- Have you tried to patch the stucco already?
- Who did you use, how does it look, and how long did it last?
- Are there any areas where dirt and grass make direct contact with stucco?
- How often are those areas watered?
- Are any sprinkler heads buried near the house itself? How often do they run them?
- Are there any areas where paint is chipping or peeling?
- Any cracks in the stucco (vertical stud cracks, horizontal foundation cracks, window/door cracks, etc).

Wood

- Do you have any wood rot on the house? If so, where?
- Have they attempted to fix it in the past?
- Who did you use, how does it look, and how long did it last?
- Are there any areas where paint is chipping or peeling?
- What is the condition of the wood underneath those areas?
- Do the eves show evidence of mold?

IN HOME SALES

As I ask the homeowner my questions, I make sure to write down their answers. Not only is this important information to have, but it also shows the potential client that I care. As I do this, I am mixing rapport building with business. Some customers are sociable and love to talk, others are more brass tax and want you to get down to business. Prospects are smarter than ever before. If you are just giving them fake rapport, cheap chit-chat, and telling them how amazing you are, you are going to be escorted to the door very quickly. The key is to ask them questions so that the prospects realize they have a need. Get them into results-based thinking over wanting a cheap fix. Listen to what they mean, not just what they say. To get better answers you need to ask better questions.

Once I have completed the warm-up it is time to go inspect the home. Remember, you must get both homeowners to go outside with you. The way I do this is a two-step process. The first step is with my words, the second one is with my body movements. So, when it is time for the inspection I will stand up, grab my clipboard, and tell them, "Well you guys know your home better than I do, why don't we go outside, and you show me the areas that concern you the most." Since I have already started moving, they are naturally going to take the cue and start heading outside with me.

Chapter 9

Inspection

The inspection is the most important part of the sales process. This is where sales are made or lost. If you cannot get the homeowners to understand the problems their home is facing, then why would they let you back inside their home to present solutions to them? Without urgency, there is no decision. The main goal of the inspections is to create need and urgency, so the homeowners realize that your solution is something they should have already done.

How you approach the inspection is critical to your success. If you're going to take the homeowners outside and tell them their house is falling apart, they will feel insulted and start giving you excuses as to why your meeting needs to end. Regardless of how bad the damage is, you must keep in mind that this is their home. For most people, their home is their largest investment and they worked and sacrificed a lot to get it. Your opinion of it does not matter. You must be tactful in how you present the information to them.

I like to think of the inspection as the doctor's approach. First, I do a lot of investigating and note-taking before I do any speaking. Second, I don't offer any solutions right away. We want to make sure to get back inside after the inspection to present our company and our solutions. If you present the wrong solutions outside, they may not let you inside to give this part of the presentation. If you offer solutions outside, it isn't necessary for you to go back inside anyway. So, my goal is to show them all the problems in a respectful manner and then get inside to present.

If at any time while I am educating them on the problems I see, they ask, "How would you fix that?"

My response would be: "Great question! There are several different ways we can take care of that. When we get inside, I'll show you your options and you can pick which one you like best. Fair enough?"

Think about going to the doctor's office. She does not give you the play-by-play as she examines you. She might note a few issues and ask some probing questions, but she will present the bad news and the plan to get you healthy again, later.

Let's look at the six rules of an inspection and then dive into each one a little deeper.

Chapter 10

Six Rules for Inspection

---

1. Take both homeowners on the inspection.
2. Inspect the entire home.
3. Kill the house and establish alarm areas.
4. Price condition using third-party stories.
5. Be a consultant: give your customers ideas about styles, colors, and options.
6. Assume the sale.

Take Both Homeowners on The Inspection

I touched upon this earlier, but to effectively close your clients on a one-call close you will have to pitch all the homeowners together. In most scenarios, this is a husband and wife. Again, if you present to one homeowner without their spouse the objection is already built in, "I need to talk to my spouse." If you present to one of them and rely on them to sell their spouse for you, it's unlikely to succeed. They will never do as good of a job of educating them on your service and product as you will.

It would help if you also had them both with you because different homeowners have different perspectives, needs, and wants. Often when you show damage to a man, he thinks he can fix it on his own (even though the damage has been there for years). At the same time, when you show the same damage to a woman, who is typically much more emotional, she will worry more about the damage and urge her husband that it needs to get done.

Having both homeowners on the exterior inspections with you also allows you to keep building rapport and establishing trust between you and the homeowners. By showing a genuine interest in their home and explaining the various aspects of the inspection, the sales rep can demonstrate their expertise and commitment to helping the homeowners find the right solution for their needs. It will also allow you to address any concerns or questions that the homeowners may have about their home, since different homeowners have different concerns. This can help build confidence and alleviate any doubts they may have about the product or service being offered.

Related to having different concerns, different homeowners will also have different objections as well. If the homeowners have any objections or hesitations about the information being presented, you can use the exterior inspection as an opportunity to overcome those objections. By addressing any concerns or doubts the homeowners may have, the sales rep can help them feel more comfortable and confident in their decision to move forward with you.

Inspect The Entire Home

It is crucial to do a complete and thorough inspection of the entire home. Inspecting the entire home allows sales representatives to make a comprehensive assessment of the home's exterior condition. This allows them to identify all areas that may need improvement and provide the homeowners with a complete solution that addresses all their needs. Often what they think is the main priority becomes the second or third priority after a professional inspection has been done. The complete inspection also leads to accurate pricing, building trust, upselling opportunities, and closing the sale.

IN HOME SALES

Accurate Pricing: By inspecting the entire home, sales representatives can accurately price their offering based on the size, condition, and specific needs of the home. This can help ensure that the homeowners receive a fair and accurate price quote that reflects the actual work that needs to be done.

Building Trust: Conducting a thorough inspection of the entire home shows to homeowners that the sales representative is committed to providing a complete and customized solution for their needs. This can help build trust and confidence in the sales representative and increase the likelihood that the homeowners will make a purchase.

Upselling Opportunities: Inspecting the entire home can also uncover additional upselling opportunities for sales representatives. By identifying other areas of the home that could benefit from their product or service, sales representatives can offer other solutions that can help maximize the value of the sale.

Closing the Sale: Inspecting the entire home allows sales representatives to create a sense of urgency and momentum toward making a purchase. By providing a complete and customized solution that addresses all of the homeowners' needs, sales representatives can help the homeowners make a more informed and confident decision to move forward with the sale.

Kill The House and Establish Alarm Areas

It is imperative to create need and urgency to make a sale that day. So, it is crucial to "establish alarm areas." Often this is best done with our vocabulary: "This looks like something that should have been done years ago." If the damage is really bad, I will tell the homeowner, "I know the office told you that the quote is available for if and when you're ready, but based on this damage I only feel comfortable giving you a quote that is good for six months. If you called the office back a year from now and the damage continues to escalate like it has, my bosses will think I didn't know what I was doing." Hopefully, they understand the severity of the damage, and taking care of it will become their number one priority.

Another one of my favorite ways to create alarm areas is simply by drawing a plot plan of the house and marking the damage in different colors. For example, if I was inspecting a home for an exterior paint job, I would draw the footprint of the house in black ink. Then I would start to label different damage in different colors. (I love the pens that have 4-6 colors in one—the pens we all had when we were kids.) So, if there was toxic mold on the house, I would mark in red ink all the areas that had toxic mold. I would mark efflorescence, commonly known as stucco cancer, in green ink. I would mark stud cracks of sill plate cracks in blue, wood rot in purple, and so on.

Later, when I'm sitting at the kitchen table with the homeowners, my plot plan would be out, and they wouldn't be able to stop themselves from staring at it. You need to keep the emotions high throughout your pitch, and the damage is on the outside, so this is a constant reminder to them that they have a lot of damage. Think back to your days in school, when you wrote a report and got it back with red ink all over it, did you generally get a good grade? Of course not. Similarly, this is a report card on the home, and the outcome is not good.

You can do this with any product that you are selling, whether it is roofing, windows, HVAC, pest control, plumbing, etc.

Price Condition Using Third-Party Stories

This step has two parts. Let's talk about the second one before the first: third-party stories. I mentioned earlier that we don't want to beat the homeowner up on the condition of their home. If you do, you just come off as a salesman, and the homeowners will begin to hate you. So how do we deliver the information to the homeowner that their damage is bad and only getting worse? We do this by telling third-party stories.

A third-party story is a sales technique that involves talking about a different customer who was in a situation similar to the one the current homeowners are in. Not only can this be done to highlight a satisfied customer, but it can also be done to illustrate the severity of the damage on the current property. The basics are to tell the homeowners that another customer was in the same situation, they understood how serious it was, and they chose to fix it. The goal of the third-party story is to educate the homeowners on the severity of their damage and the consequences of doing nothing without beating them up. The third-party story is also used to establish credibility and build trust with the potential customer by demonstrating the real-world benefits and positive outcomes that others have experienced from using the product or service. This can be particularly effective in situations where the potential customer is skeptical or unsure about the product or service being offered.

By telling third-party stories you are also raising your stock. You are indirectly telling the homeowner that you have experience and that other families have chosen to work with you. The more experience you have, the more comfortable someone will be working with you.

The price conditioning part of third-party stories is crucial. Price conditioning is the process of preparing a customer for the price of a product or service before telling them the actual price. This is important because it avoids giving the potential client sticker shock—it is exceedingly difficult to get the customer back once that happens.

Price conditioning can be done in a variety of ways, but I find it is most effective through third-party stories when discussing other projects similar to the one you are pitching to the clients. The goal of price conditioning is to help customers understand the value of what they are buying and to avoid surprises when they see the final price. By doing so, customers are more likely to feel comfortable with the price and less likely to feel the need to negotiate or walk away from the sale.

I have always taught my sales reps to have a third-party story scripted out for every damage that they may find in a home. This way they are free to think about their client and not the story. The more you practice your story the more natural it will come off when delivered.

There is never a wrong time to tell a third-party story. Yes, they are part of the sales process, and they are highly effective in educating your client on the damage to their home. But there are many other ways to use them. They can be used in your company story, product demo, or even during closing. For example, if you are introducing financing to a client, instead of telling them, "We have finance options," or "Let's put you on a payment plan for so many months," it is more relatable to tell them a story of another client you helped who was in a comparable situation. They chose to take care of things with monthly installment options and got the job done.

The ingredients to a third-party story include: name, location, scenario (problem/solution), price conditioning, and a tie-down. We use names and locations because it makes it personal. It shows that you remember your customers and care about them. The scenario relates to whatever it is you are talking to them about. Make sure to tell the homeowner the consequences of the scenario through your story. Price condition your client higher than what you know you will price them at. And finally, tie them down. A tie-down is a form of getting the homeowner to take ownership of the problem and agree with you. Remember what you say does not matter—you are the sales rep. However, what they say is their reality. So, if they agree that the problem has to be fixed, then it's their idea to fix it, and they are more likely to act.

If I was looking at a wall full of vertical cracks, I would ask the client: "Do you know what this is? How long has it been going on? How would you go about fixing this?" Then I would educate them on what's really going on. "What we are looking at here is a stud crack in your stucco. Are you familiar with how a house is framed? Well basically you have our concrete foundation, and then on top of that, they put a thick wooden beam called a sill plate. Attached to your sill plate they put studs every 16 inches apart. I am sure you have seen a house being framed. Then after the framing, they put up sheeting, moisture barrier, chicken wire, then three layers of stucco. Unfortunately, stucco is very porous, and it absorbs moisture. So, what is happening here is your wooden studs are drinking the water that the stucco is absorbing. Do you know what happens to wood when it gets wet?"

This is the perfect place to then go into a third-party story:

"This reminds me a lot of Jake and Joan LeFleur in Costa Mesa. They had the same thing happening on two of their walls. You could see where every single stud was on their wall because the studs got wet and then the water cracked the stucco to escape. If you were to take an X-ray of a body you would see bones, if you were to take an X-ray of a home you would see studs. Well, Jake and Joan's wall got so bad that one of their studs ended up buckling, like a knee or an elbow. You could push on the wall. We just wanted to break the stucco where the stud broke, but the city inspector made us break the stucco from corner to corner. Not only did he make us replace the broken stud, but he also had us replace three to the right and three to the left for the structural integrity of the wall. Then we had to put new sheeting, moisture barrier, chicken wire, and three layers of stucco. It ended up costing them over $28,000 before they picked a color. Can we agree that whether my company does it or another company does it, this has to get fixed?"

So instead of beating them up about all the problems they are facing, I indirectly give them all that information in the form of a third-party story. Also, notice the tie-down that I used. Would you ever suggest using a different contractor other than yourself? Why would I say that? The main reason is that I don't want to come off as desperate and I don't want them to feel that I am a pushy salesperson. I am a good guy who wants to educate the homeowners and allow them to make the best decision for them. The other reason is that I am extremely confident in my presentation and myself and know that saying things like this will allow them to be confident and honest with me.

Be A Consultant: Give Your Customers Ideas About Styles, Colors, Options

While walking around the home, identifying damage and continuing to build rapport with the homeowners, it is a good idea to act as a consultant. I ask questions about color, facades, and woodwork. If discussing paint, I ask questions about the windows, the patio covering, etc. Often, I will just ask a question, give them a brochure on the other product we are talking about, and move on. This is part of "seeding" a reload. A reload means coming back later and selling another product. A lot of reps like to hit home runs and write up huge orders on the first visit. I prefer to write nice healthy orders from day one and then come back and add more to them later.

It is easier to get a "yes" on a single project instead of a bunch of different projects lumped together. It also proves to the homeowner that I'm not a sales monster and makes buyer's remorse less likely.

Assume The Sale

Your behavior and language are what will help you when assuming the sale. Ask questions as if you've already been hired: "Will you guys be removing the cameras on the fascia boards, or do you want my crew to do it?" "Are you guys okay with us cutting these hedges back a little bit so my guys can get in there to work."

If you can get the homeowner to select styles, options, and colors, and agree to all the details regarding the work, they are indicating that they also assume you will be doing the project.

Once I do a complete exterior inspection of the home, I tell the homeowner that I'm going to walk around the home one more time and get some measurements. Most of the time they will leave you alone and go back inside. However, if they want to stay and watch, by all means, it is their home.

After the measurements, I go to my car and get everything necessary to make the sale inside at the kitchen table. This includes samples, and anything else I might need to carry me through. I do not want to have to step out to the car again later, as the task now is to sit at the kitchen table until my work orders are signed, financing is in place if needed, and I have a deposit in hand.

Once I'm back inside from my inspection, I like to take a few minutes and show my prospective client some completed job files on my computer. I'll open a file and tell them, "Remember those stud cracks you had on your north wall, well here are those same cracks on Margret and Bill's house. Here are the before, during, and after photos." I will do this with three to four files, making sure to show houses that have similar issues to the ones they are facing. They can see that they are not the only ones with these issues, the people that had them chose to hire me, and the completed photos look incredible.

Going through the photos also allows me to highlight the detailed work and clean job site that my crew keeps. I am also raising my stock, showing them that I visit my customers and I have a lot of experience in the industry. Remember a picture tells a thousand words. Show pictures!

IN HOME SALES

Chapter 11

Set the Stage

Once I have shown them a few photos, I will then set the stage. Some call this "step the preframe." Regardless of what you call it, the point of it is to give the homeowners a syllabus for the rest of the meeting.

"Mr./Mrs. _____, I look at my job as three-fold.

First I'd like to tell you about myself and the company so you feel comfortable doing business with us. Next, I'll show you the materials we use and the care we take to prepare your home for installation. Then, I'm going to give you an exact quote in writing. When I'm done you'll have to ask yourself three questions.

Do you like me and the benefits my company has to offer?

Is our material what you want on the exterior of your home?

And lastly, is it comfortably affordable for you and your family?

If your answer is yes to all three, I'm here to take an order today, if not we can shake hands and part as friends. FAIR ENOUGH?"

Setting the stage like this accomplishes several things. First and foremost, it indirectly tells the homeowner that they will not get a price from me until after I have done a complete presentation. Second, it lets them know that I will be asking for their business today. You have to remember that many of these appointments are set up as free inspections. If an appointment is just a free inspection, but then I try to close the homeowner at the end, it just looks like a bait and switch. By telling them that I will be asking for their business, they know what to expect. It changes the tone of the meeting from one of a free inspection to one of business.

One of my favorite parts about setting the stage is that when you finish with your tie down ("fair enough?"), the homeowner will often take that opportunity to give you their objection. The reason this is amazing is that I haven't asked for the order, so they are showing me their cards an hour and a half before I really ask for their business. By telling me what their objection is going to be, I can indirectly combat it until we get to the close. It is as if someone showed me their poker hand before I made my bet.

It is important to note, that no matter what their objections are, my response will always be a smile and a "no problem." Never respond to their objection and try to close it right then. Just deflect it and move on. If you talk about it or try to close it at that moment, all you are doing is empowering their objection.

Once the stage is set and everyone is on the same page as far as what to expect for the rest of our meeting, I then move on to the company story.

IN HOME SALES

Chapter 12

Company Story

Regardless of how many homeowners tell you it doesn't matter, or they already looked you up, telling the company story is a crucial step that cannot be skipped. There is a lot of closing that happens here, without them knowing. Every step of my process is getting me closer to a "yes" at the end. Anything I skip can come back and bite me in the ass later.

The company story is much more than telling my prospect how amazing our company is. This is where you differentiate yourself from the industry standard companies that do what you do. This is also where you build trust and value in your company. Often you are answering questions the homeowner has before they even know it's an important question to ask.

IN HOME SALES

The company story is usually done with PowerPoint or Keynote, using an iPad or laptop. The point of the slides is to have a visual for a homeowner and the key talking points laid out. It is not your job to read each slide out to the homeowner, your job is to tell them everything the slide does not say, and to explain to them why it's important. Every time I teach my sales representatives the company story, after presenting each slide I say, "So what?" or "What's in it for me?" If your slide is not making a critical point or educating the homeowner on something they need to know, then you are wasting both your time and, more importantly, their time.

Your company story should consist of things like licenses, bonds, and insurance. What do you have versus the industry standard? When I say, "industry standard," I'm talking about every regular shmo in your field. Contractors have a difficult job when it comes to sales. Every homeowner you talk to has either been screwed by one or knows someone that has. So, you're already starting in a negative position.

Generally, people associate contractors with dirty boots, dirty trucks, bad attitudes, and drugs and alcohol. Most contractors do not go through any of the steps we are discussing in this book. They just show up to the job, look at the job, and write a price on a piece of paper. Or they may just tell the homeowner that they'll get back to them. What's amazing is how many of them never even reach out to give the homeowner the estimate, despite taking the time and wasting the gas to go see the job. It's crucial to separate yourself from the industry standard and make your prospect feel at ease and comfortable, with the knowledge that they are dealing with a professional. By doing this, you eliminate one of the most common objections of the homeowner—wanting to get other bids.

Throughout the pitch, you should indirectly close the homeowner, trying to eliminate all objections other than price. Many sales professionals rush the presentation and try to muscle the close. I work the other way around, methodically moving through these steps, and trying to narrow down the objection to money. It is much easier to close the money objection than all the other arbitrary objections such as wanting to get other bids, talking to a third party, different priorities, etc. Even though I am narrowing it down to money, my goal is still to create as much value as possible.

The goal is for the prospect to think that the price you will give them will be higher than what you quote them. If they think the price is going to be more than what you quote, not only did you do a phenomenal job creating value, the homeowner is pleasantly surprised and your close will be easier than normal.

The company story should be filled with value. Not only should you be separating yourself from the industry standard, but you should also be giving the homeowners valuable information that others would be unlikely to share. For example, in California where I live no contractor is allowed to take a deposit greater than ten percent or $1000, whichever is less. Most homeowners are unaware of this. There have been numerous times that I have told a homeowner this, and they respond by telling me that the kitchen guy or the bathroom guy from a previous project asked for a much larger deposit.

    Even if they do not hire me, this practice sends the message that I know my stuff and that I'm a good person. You may not close these homeowners today, which is part of the game, but you also don't know who they know. They may not buy from you, but they may like you and trust you and refer you to a friend, coworker, or family member. Doing the right thing is always the right thing.

    A lot of the information I teach the homeowners during my company presentation is also done through third-party stories. The phrase "facts tell, stories sell" is a famous quote in the world of sales. As the saying suggests, to sell, you need to give potential purchasers a reason to act. A story emotionalizes information, fuels connection, and is more engaging than just providing data and facts.

    Telling your homeowner stories also humanizes you and your company. It reveals that there are real people behind the company, people with fears, passions, vulnerabilities, struggles, and successes. A good story will capture your homeowners' attention and hold it to the end. Whatever point you are trying to convey will hit home much better with a relevant story than merely with facts.

No one likes to have facts hurled at them. Teach your customers about your unique company and how it makes their lives easier or better through stories instead. When customers are engaged in your story, they will learn about your company and come to appreciate it without realizing that you are educating them. Understanding will come naturally through the flow of your story. This must be done in a smooth, conversational way. When telling your stories you should also consider what questions the homeowner may ask you and how you might respond. If caught off guard, this may derail the story altogether.

It is of the utmost importance that you ask your homeowner tie-down questions after almost every slide. This ensures that they are listening to you and engaged, while still keeping the presentation conversational. Even though you are giving a presentation, you do not want to lecture your client. The conversation should be about 65% you and 35% them. Ask them questions you already know the answer to, just to keep them engaged and agreeing with you. As I mentioned before, what you say doesn't matter as much as what they hear themselves say.

What exactly is a tie-down question? In sales, a tie-down question is a type of question that a salesperson uses to confirm or solidify a prospect's agreement or commitment to a product or service. These questions are typically closed-ended, meaning they require a simple "yes" or "no" answer, and they are designed to help the salesperson move the conversation forward and close the sale.

Tie-down questions are useful because they help the salesperson gauge the prospect's level of interest and commitment and identify any objections or concerns that need to be addressed. Additionally, tie-down questions can help build rapport and establish trust between the salesperson and the prospect by showing that the salesperson is actively listening and responding to the prospect's needs and preferences. Tie-down questions can be simple. For example:

"Safe to say _____?"
"Fair enough?"
"Are you with me?"

They are most effectively delivered when your tone goes up at the end of your question.

As I am stressing the importance of having a conversation with the homeowner and not simply lecturing them, there are other questions that you can ask besides tie-down questions. One of my favorite questions that I start my company story with is, "Tom and Nancy, when you are looking to hire a contractor what are some of the most important things to you?" With this question, I'm asking my homeowner to tell me what I have to say to close them. Naturally, I write down their responses to make sure I hit all their points at the end of my company story. Once they tell me what is important to them, I know which parts of my company story I need to emphasize more than others to these particular people.

My slides for the company story always consist of the following: license, bond, and insurance. These are terms that everyone throws around, but not many people know what they mean. So, I will educate them on my license, what it allows me to do, and how it is safer to work with me than some other guy who does not have one. I will cover the repercussions of working with someone without a license, and then I will ask them a tie-down question. It's the same overall process with bond and insurance.

From there my company story will go on to other licenses such as city licenses and permits, if applicable. I will show them where my company stands with the Contractors State License Board and other government agencies, again stressing the difference between my company and other companies that do not have all their i's dotted and t's crossed.

This is also the time to educate the homeowner on how my company is a real company and not a "one-man band" working out of a garage or truck. The following questions can be addressed: Why is it important to work with a company that has a physical office rather than one operating out of a truck? Why is it important to work with a company with a customer service department? What does my production department do, and how does it affect the end user?

My production department communicates with the homeowner starting the very next day that they sign their contract. We give them a welcome call and introduce ourselves to them. We set up their sight survey with the crew supervisor, who will be responsible for their job. We then communicate with them their start date. Once we are on-site, we communicate with them every single day about what is going on at their property, ensuring that all their questions are answered. Few other companies do this, but it is important that the customer know the level of service that you and your company will provide. This is creating massive value for the homeowner.

At this stage of the presentation, I also talk about our crews and who they are. Although my company sells a lot of different exterior products, my roofers only do roofing, my window installers only install windows, and my painters only paint. Instead of having workers who are jacks of all trades and masters of none, we only work with people who specialize in their respective craft. This ensures much better installations and increases customer satisfaction. Another thing I share about our company is how we sell a lot of volume. Since we sell a lot of volume we get better pricing from our manufacturers, which we then pass on to our clients. These are key details to share with our potential customers.

While discussing how my company is set up, I make sure to contrast this with how other companies are set up to highlight the dangers of working with smaller contractors. The guy who acts as a one-man operation may be a little cheaper, but what is the risk? If he runs out of material, he needs to leave your job to go buy it. If the phone rings for an estimate, he needs to leave your job to ensure he has another one when he completes this one. If the day gets away from him and he needs to go to the bank before closing, he is going to leave your job to go to the bank. He doesn't have enough bandwidth to go back to jobs when he is trying to create new income to survive. Small guys generally do not offer the homeowner financing options. With them cash is king, if you have the money they can do the job, if you do not, then you have to call them when you do. These one-person operations often give a low bid to make sure they get the contract, but as time goes on, they give you the mid-job knock. They may also tell you they will install a particular product, but ultimately pull a bait-and-switch on you to maximize their small profit. Then there is the lack of customer service with these barebone operations.

Once I paint a very clear picture between the small guy and an operation like mine, which is set up like a company, it is crucial to get the buy-in from the homeowner with a tie down questions such as, "Which type of company would give

IN HOME SALES

you greater peace of mind to work with, the little guy or a company like mine?"

I then move on to our relationship with each of our manufacturers. Regardless of what product I am currently pitching, I will talk about all of them. This allows me to seed my reload. A reload is going back to the same homeowner and selling them another product.

I never want to sell more than one product on the first visit. While a lot of reps like to do it and land the "whale," my philosophy is that it is more productive and profitable to sell one product at a time. The homeowners will also see you as more trustworthy than a guy who wants to take all their money for a bunch of different projects. Another problem with trying to sell a whale is that the homeowner may have a budget. If, for example, they have $20,000 budgeted for a new roof and then you bring up their exterior paint, they may then try to get both items done for the same budget. It's better to sell one at that time, sell the next in the future, and increase my earnings on the job.

Another important detail to include in the company story is review sights. What does the public have to say about you? Google, Yelp, and the Better Business Bureau are all great sites that can help your company's image. Generally, reviewing those sites is something a homeowner will do anyway, so it is better to review them together, while you are there than to let them do it on their own later. God forbid they find something they question or do not like, if you are no longer there, there is nothing you can do about it.

Remember the entire point of this is to sell your company to your potential client. If your company has received any honorable mentions or awards, these are great to add to your company story. We make sure to mention that we can help our customers with monthly installments and have a slide about our partners who can facilitate this. There is also a slide showing which credit cards we accept. Remember a lot of companies do not accept credit cards, and the fact that you do will give you an advantage. Not only does the homeowner not need to have all the cash saved up, they can take care of their home and get points or mileage at the same time.

As I wrap up my company story I always ask three tie-down questions before moving on:

"After everything I shared with you about XYZ company, are we a company you would feel comfortable working with?"

"Great, what stood out to you about XYZ company?"

"So we are the company for you?"

I am asking the homeowner a close-ended question, followed by an open-ended question, followed by a closed-ended question. It is important to make sure that the homeowner is sold on the company before telling them about the product. I would hate to get to the end and hear the homeowner tell me they need to do more research on my company.

These questions accomplish a few obvious and some not-so-obvious things. First and foremost, they provide a report card for you on your presentation. If they tell you they need to research your company further or are not sure about working with your company, you know you need to go back to the office and role-play your company story with one of your peers. Maybe it was too one-sided or was lacking some critical education. Maybe there were not enough tie-downs for the homeowner to buy in.

The other thing that these questions do for you is move the prospect along the sales process. The most important of the three questions is the second one, in which the prospect is essentially closing themselves. I make sure to get responses from all the homeowners who are participating in the presentation. They should close themselves and each other at the same time.

Once I assure myself that the homeowner is comfortable with the company, it is time to move on to the product demonstration. Again, in my world, this is done with a Keynote presentation and has physical samples to go along with it. If I were demonstrating a roof, I would have not only the shingles, underlayment, starter strip, edge metal, and other key ingredients that I sell, but I would also have the industry standard samples as well. My goal is for the homeowner to visualize, touch, and feel the industry standard material and process versus mine. So let's dive deeper into the product demo.

IN HOME SALES

Chapter 13

Product Demo

The product demonstration is an essential aspect of selling home improvements because it allows potential customers to see the product in action, experience its benefits, and understand its features. A product demonstration can help build confidence in the product and make it easier for customers to make a buying decision. I am a firm believer that the homeowner has to see, touch, and feel the materials they are purchasing for their home.

I have had amazing sales representatives in the past sell homeowners' windows without them ever physically seeing the windows. Most of the time the process went okay, but there have been a couple of instances when the homeowner hated the window they had just bought because they never got to see it. They didn't like the amount of vinyl that was showing around the frame, or they didn't like the style of the lock that was on the window.

Problems like these can easily be avoided by doing a proper product demonstration with the homeowner. They are done for the same reason people want to test drive a car before they buy it. A product demonstration can help customers understand the features and benefits of the product and how it can address their specific needs or concerns. This can be especially important for projects designed to improve the comfort or energy efficiency of the home. Not only should the homeowner know every benefit and feature of your product, they should know how the material will be installed in their home and how your company's method is the best way possible to get it done.

Another reason for the product demo is it helps customers visualize the end result. A product demonstration can help customers envision what their home will look like after the improvement is made. This can be especially important for home improvements that require a significant investment or that have a major impact on the appearance of the home. This is when we are sparking the homeowner's emotions! Along with helping them visualize the product, demonstrating it to them can help build trust with the customer by showing that the product is effective and delivers on its promises.

Teaching your homeowner about the material also provides an opportunity for customers to ask questions and provide feedback. This, in turn, helps the salesperson tailor their pitch to better meet the customer's needs. It can also be especially important for home improvements that are more complex or require a higher level of expertise.

In order to be a sales professional and close at a very high level you need to know the product inside and out. Salespeople need to have a deep understanding of the product they are demonstrating, including its features, benefits, and potential drawbacks. This will allow the salesperson to answer questions confidently and provide detailed information about the product. Also, a high level of knowledge will help a salesperson tailor the presentation to the specific needs and preferences of the customer. For example, if the customer is interested in energy efficiency, the demonstration should focus on that aspect of the product. If they are concerned with something like toxic mold, explain to them the features of your material and how it will cure it and prevent it from coming back.

It would help if you made this part of the presentation interactive. Rather than simply showing the product, salespeople should consider allowing the customer to handle or try the product themselves. This can help build engagement and investment in the product.

IN HOME SALES

It is also imperative that you practice and refine the demonstration. Salespeople should practice their product demonstration in advance and seek feedback from colleagues or managers to refine their approach. This can help ensure that the demonstration is polished and effective in driving sales.

Generally, when building my product demonstration keynote presentation, I like to start by making sure that I have a few slides that will affect the homeowners' emotions. They were emotional when we inspected the outside of the home as we reviewed the damage. Then we went inside, sat at the kitchen table, set the stage, and did the company story. Often during these steps, all the emotions that you activated outside have begun to settle. So, I want to remind them about their damage.

In my exterior paint presentation, I start with the reason people paint. I list them all out and ask the client, "Out of all these reasons to paint your house Mr. And Mrs. Jones, what are your top reasons?" Remember it is more effective for me to have them tell me their pain points than for me to tell them what they are. Then I have a few slides that discuss what the damages are and what causes them. It is key to hit the damages they have harder than the ones they don't. Remember we are looking to get a "yes" from them today!

It's the same process with other products as well. With a roof repair, my product demo starts with reasons why people replace their roofs. I go over each reason and the consequence of each one, reminding them that these are the same problems we saw on their roof. If you don't relate these problems to them, then you are just going through a presentation that has no meaning or real importance to them.

Once I have stirred their emotion back up and got them thinking about their problems, I start to talk about the process of how the job is going to get done. If there are permits required, I let them know about them and assure the homeowners that we will take care of them. I then separate us from the industry standard and the average Joe, who either fails to tell the homeowner they need a permit or fails to pull one for the homeowner. This is another opportunity to teach the homeowners about laws and regulations, something most representatives do not do. This in turn reflects well on me and my company and shows that I am an expert in this field.

Then I show slides of every single step of the process, differentiating how my company does them compared to the industry standard. For example, when it comes to tearing off a roof, a lot of roofers will simply grab some pitchforks and flat shovels and start tearing the roof off. All the material gets thrown down to the ground and a crew member is responsible for shoveling it all into a wheelbarrow and putting it into a dumpster. The problem is that this process creates a huge mess! The average roof has 9,000 to 12,000 nails in it. There can also be toxic mold on the shingles that is being activated when thrown off the roof, contaminating the air coming into the home. My slides include a few pictures of this and the mess this creates at someone's house.

Then I proceed to talk about how my company tears off a roof. We have a large dump truck that backs up into your driveway and up to the roofline. If necessary, we have a bridge that connects the roof and truck. So, as we are removing your roof the material goes directly from the roof, into the truck, avoiding the huge mess that other companies create. At the end of the process, we have a four-foot magnetic roller that we roll around the entire perimeter of the home to make sure we clean up any nails or staples that may have fallen. My slideshow includes photos showing all of this.

Besides automatically looking better than most companies, we look more professional and can build more value. The more value you can build during your presentation, the more a homeowner will be willing to pay for your service. Homeowners do not want the cheapest, they want the person who delivers the most value for them, and the one who can get it done professionally.

After the tear-off, the discussion would move into wood replacement. Most roofers bamboozle homeowners by not giving them clear expectations of what will happen at that stage. They often do not discuss wood replacement with a homeowner and simply knock on the door asking for more money once the roof is torn off. How do you think this makes a homeowner feel? They are paying $23,000 for their roof, thinking that it is all-inclusive, and then their contractor goes back to them asking for two, three, or even ten thousand dollars more for wood replacement.

So instead of blindsiding my homeowner with this information, I prepare them for it during my initial presentation. "This is what a roof looks like when it is torn off. Some roofs need a lot of wood replacement, and some do not. Unfortunately, we will not know how much wood replacement you will need until it is torn off. This is the only thing, that is not included in the price I give you today. It is not fair to the company to charge you for ten feet when you may end up needing a hundred; and it is not fair to charge you for one hundred feet when you may end up needing only ten. So, we charge x amount of dollars per linear foot, and when the roof is torn off, I will be more than happy to show you all the wood that has been replaced. Fair enough?"

If there is any chance that they got a quote from another roofer who did not disclose this, which most do not, then again, your stock went up. The other guys just lost the business because they did not give an accurate description of all the work to be done and the costs associated with it. A lot of sales representatives are under the impression that what they do not say will not hurt them. I disagree—say everything and sell with integrity.

IN HOME SALES

Next, I discuss the manufacturer: who they are, what they stand for, and why I choose to work with them. From there, I go step by step through the installation process. This is the chance to show them how we do it versus how the industry standard does it and tie down each thought before continuing to the next.

As I am showing the slides on my computer, I am also bringing out the related materials. So, for roofing, I literally build two roofs on their kitchen table: the industry standard roof, with common materials, and the roof I sell with each component on it. If the slides are not painting a clear enough picture, oftentimes the physical samples will.

From there I show a lot of before and after pictures. Generally, my before and after photos are labeled with the homeowner's last name, the city, and the price. This again helps me show that I have a lot of customers, and people trust me and do business with me. It also helps me price condition the potential client sitting in front of me. I also like to show company stats on how many jobs we have done and those pending. Once I have completed my product demonstration, I move on to the Today Page.

Chapter 14

Today Page

Although this is generally the last page of my product demo, I make the "today page" its very own step in the sales process because it is so important to getting that final "yes" on that day. While we use tie-down questions at the end of the company story and product demo, this page is all tie-downs. This page will provide you with your true report card on how you did, and how the homeowners perceive you and your company.

Besides finding out how good your presentation skills are, this page also allows you to know the key takeaways that your homeowner grasped from each step. It allows the homeowners to close themselves and each other. And most importantly, it funnels down their objections to money.

IN HOME SALES

Remember, the money objection is easier to close than all the other arbitrary ones.

As with all sales, the vocabulary you use is just as important as how you deliver the words. So I start by saying, "When making your decision today, these are the most important things to consider." Notice that I use the word "today." We are getting a decision from our homeowner today! Then I go back to the same format we mentioned before—a close-ended question, followed by an open-ended question, followed by a closed-ended question.

Here is what the page looks like: "When making your decision today, here are some of the most important things to consider ..."

1. Company

"Is my company a company you would feel comfortable working with?" "Great, what are some of the things that stood out to you about my company?" "So safe to say we are the company for you and your family?"

2. Product

"As far as the XYZ material, is this a material you can see on your home?" "What about it did you like?" "So this is the material for you?"

3. Warranty

"As far as the lifetime warranty, is that long enough?" "What did you like about it?" "Is this the type of warranty that would give you peace of mind?"

4. Representative

"Do you feel I was able to educate you on the condition of your home and your options?" "Great, do you feel I can make this project come to fruition for you and your family?" "Thank you. I have really enjoyed my time with you today."

5. Investment

"So, it sounds to me like you like the company, you love the material, and both the warranty and I check out. It sounds like it just comes down to the dollar and cents. If I can show you a price that is fair and affordable, I would love to take your order today. Fair enough?"

Now we smile and wait for them to respond. Often they say, "Sure, let's see what the number are." Sometimes they may give you an objection. If they do, we just acknowledge them, say "no problem," and move on. They still do not know the price, so this is not when you try and close them.

Now that we have gone through the "today page," let's examine why we do it and what we are accomplishing. The most important reason for it is to narrow down the objection to money. I am a pretty lazy closer and want to make the closing process as easy as possible for myself. If I can eliminate all the usual nonsense that homeowners throw out such as, "we'll think about it," or "we want to seek out more bids," then I can spend more time creating a deal or finding a payment plan the homeowner is comfortable with and close.

Another reason to go through the "today page" is simply to see how your presentation went. This is a litmus test for your presentation. I will ask the homeowner, "After everything I shared with you, are we the type of company that you feel comfortable working with?" If they tell me that they need to do some more research on my company, then my company story was clearly not as strong as I would like it to be. I will need to go back to the office and role-play my company story. Maybe it was too one-sided and I did not separate my company from industry standards. Maybe I didn't ask enough tie-down questions to make sure the homeowner was following along

The same can be said about the product or the warranty. I will ask the homeowner, "Is this the material you want to see on the outside of your home?" If they respond that they want to see what other options they have, then I have failed to present the homeowner with all the possible options and distinguish why my option was the best.

Another reason to go through the "today page" is so that the homeowners can hear each other say "yes" to my company, product, warranty, and representative. Along with them saying "yes," the second question in each of the sequences, asking what they liked about the company, product, or warranty, allows them to close themselves and each other. Remember, I can tell them all the reasons everything is great, but it is far more powerful for them to list the reasons themselves, and to hear each other's reasons. Not only are they closing themselves, but they are also closing each other.

    Once I have gone through the "today page" sequence, it comes down to that last line, where I summarize it all up and let them know that it comes down to the money: "If I can show you a price that is fair and affordable I would love to take your order today. Fair enough?" Again, you may get a "yes" or an objection. Either way we move on to the next step.

IN HOME SALES

Chapter 15

Passing Price with the Work Order

Before I show the customers the price, which is really all they wanted since I got there, I want to review everything we've gone over thus far and continue to build as much value as possible. One of the best ways to accomplish this is by doing a work order review with them. Before showing them the price, I go line by line over a blank work order. Remember vocabulary matters, and a lot of representatives say the word "contract" instead of "work order." Even though a work order is a contract, the word "contract" is very intimidating to homeowners, and often they may want to have their lawyer review it before signing. However, homeowners have no fear of work orders, and everything continues to move forward smoothly.

There are several reasons to review the work order with them before passing the price. First and foremost, they see that everything you have been talking about today is in writing. Long gone are the days of taking someone's word, shaking hands, and saying, "See you Monday." Everything must be written out for the homeowner to see. If by any chance they missed something in your presentation, they will get to see it at this stage. They also need to be familiar with what you are asking them to sign. If their first time seeing the work order is after you give them the price and ask them to sign, then all your momentum is going to come to a sudden halt. They are going to want to review what they are signing, and that emotional momentum you have will end. However, if they have already seen the work order and are familiar with it, as soon as you agree on the price, they can sign and you can get a sale.

So, after I do the "today page," I tell the homeowner, "Let me show you in writing exactly what it is you are getting today." We go through the work order line by line, top to bottom. "As you can see, here is our company name, our license number, address, and phone number. Down below we will fill out all your contact information. Please double-check the address so we do not accidentally rip off our neighbor's roof. Then there is a breakdown of everything we will be doing to your home." Make sure to relate each line item to their project and needs. I go down the entire scope of work, all the way down to the signatures. "I sign here. You will sign there. Fair enough?"

The other thing accomplished by going over the work order is to take away the fear of the work order. It is normalized and is no longer a scary document to the homeowner. If you fail to go over the work order and whip it out after you have given the customer the price, they will start to bark at it. They will say things like, "What is that for?" or "We won't be signing anything today, you can put that away."

So before showing them their investment, I go over the work order and review my plot plan and pictures of the damage to their home. I want to stir the cauldron of emotion and remind them that they have damage to their home that needs fixing. Now I am prepared to share their investment with them.

Before showing them the number, I always start by forecasting positivity. "Jon and Mary I worked up the number, and they really worked out in your favor, I don't see any reason why we would not be taking care of this today." I am very cool, calm, and collected when saying this, while smiling. The alternative would be to project anything negative about the investment we are asking for. "Man this is a lot, I hope you guys can afford this." That would obviously be a disastrous way to approach the situation. If I have done my presentation properly, presented plenty of third-party stories with price conditioning, created need, and done an excellent job with my company story and product demo, the homeowner should feel that the investment I am about to present them is going to be higher than what it is.

As I present the investment to my potential clients the vocabulary used is very important. The amount the homeowners are paying will be minimized and the savings will be emphasized. Before we dive deeper into this let me show you a sample of my passing price form.

SHAI ADES

Owner

Job Address

AREA	HOW MANY (# OR FT)
Composite	30
Designer	0
Overlay	0
Flat	0
Tile Lift/Reset	0
New Tile	0
Layer 2 remove	30
Layer 3 remove	0
Layer 4 remove	0
1/2 redecking	0
Ln ft ridge vent	74
remove reinstall solar	0
chimney skylight	0

AREA	HOW MANY (# OR FT)
steep pitch	0
poor access	0
cover pool	0
fascia replacement	0
rafter tail replacement	0
plywood replacement	0
gutters	0
insulation cleanout	0
new insulation	0
permits	1
warranty	1
wastage	1

Manufacturer Rebates
3

Discount Code
hero10

APPLY

You have successfully used the "Local Heroes Discount" discount

Sub Total	$49,628.00
Manufacturers Rebate	$1,500.00
Discounts (10%):	-$4,962.80
Total work order price:	$43,165.20

Option A
Deposit	$1,000.00
Progress Payment	$12,949.56
Completion	$29,215.64

Option B
Deposit	$1,000.00
Monthly Installment	$843.30 - $1,264.96

IN HOME SALES

So if the initial investment before discounts would be $32,946.00, I would present this as: "The entire project came out to ONLY thirty-two nine forty-six." Notice I never used the word "thousand."

Then there would be some form of incentive for the homeowner to act today, such as three $500 manufacturer credits. I would present this as, "Currently we have teamed up with our manufacturer to increase our orders and we are offering you three $500 rebates to be deducted from the total price today. This is not like the old Radio Shack rebates that you sent in the mail, and sometimes you got them and sometimes you did not. We will deduct ONE THOUSAND FIVE HUNDRED DOLLARS off your total investment today. So, today your investment is only thirty-one, four forty-six." Again, notice how the payments the homeowners are going to be making sound small, communicated without using words like "thousand."

We then move down the page and into the different payment options. Option A would be a credit card or check, and option B would be the monthly installment option. The way I would present these options is as follows: "Option A is your credit card or check option. It would be a small thousand-dollar deposit, a 30% progress payment once the job is started, and the final balance at the end of the project when you don't even recognize your house. Option B would be the same thousand-dollar deposit and a monthly installment between X amount of dollars and X amount of dollars. Which option works best for you?" I would then hand over the pricing form to the homeowner and turn my attention to filling out the work order.

What you say once you present the numbers is crucial. You don't want to ask things like, "What do you think about that?" or "Do you want to do it?" You simply want to present the investment to the homeowner and ask which option works best, or even better, "Will the deposit be a credit card or check?" Then, SHUT UP! Let them digest the information for a minute and think. Sometimes they are moving money around in their heads or trying to sort financials out. You don't want to take away from this. Remember they have been waiting for these numbers for two and a half to three hours. So we just want to give them the numbers and ask if they prefer option A or option B, or if their deposit will be by credit card or check.

Regardless of how well your presentation went, you are more than likely going to receive an objection from a homeowner. It is very rare for a homeowner to simply say "yes," even if they want to do it. Following a likely objection, it is imperative that you remain cool, calm, and collected through your closing. Remember the entire time you have been at their house you have been trying to show them that you are not a sales monster and that you genuinely care about them and their property. You do not want to throw that all away so close to the end.

IN HOME SALES

It is helpful to change how you think about such objections. They are not inherently negative. On the contrary, they can indicate a prospect's genuine interest in moving forward. Often, they simply need more information, or require a connection between concepts, to gain a clearer understanding. So, whenever I encounter an objection, I respond with empathy and a smile and say, "I completely understand and appreciate that." This approach not only addresses their concerns but also smoothly transitions us from discussing pricing to entering the closing phase of the sale.

Chapter 16

Closing

That empathy statement lets the homeowners know that I understand how they are feeling. It is the statement I always use when there is an objection leading into closing. As a trained, sales professional, I do not want to wing my empathy statement, so I'm always ready for this. It is always a smile followed by, "I can understand and appreciate that." This allows the homeowner to put down their guard, and feel heard, and understood.

There are many sales courses out there that will teach you to question the homeowner or to try and pin the objection to the homeowner before trying to overcome it. By doing this, you are doing yourself a disservice and empowering the objection. It also may irritate the homeowner for you to ask them to elaborate on their objection. I simply acknowledge their objection with an empathy statement, and then move on. More often than not the objection the homeowner spits out is not even the real objection. So, if it is not the real objection why would we empower it and add a roadblock to our close?

So, we move on and I ask, "When do you think I should follow up with you folks, a couple of days, weeks, months?" By asking them when I should follow up, I give the homeowners room to breathe and put their guard down. They are under the impression that I am backing down and getting ready to leave. Really, I am simply getting them to relax. Closing is a constant equilibrium of pressure on and pressure off.

Before I start preparing to negotiate or drop my price I will ask the homeowner, "I don't know if I can, but if I were able to do something about the deposit or the monthly installment, would I be able to earn your business today?" Sometimes the homeowners are in a predicament where they love everything, but the $1000 deposit is just not feasible today. Instead of simply telling you that, they give you a smoke screen like, "we need to think about it," to avoid embarrassment. Maybe they get paid next week and they are strapped for extra cash for a couple of days. Or maybe the monthly installment is simply a little out of their comfort zone, but again they are too embarrassed to speak up and tell you. By asking this simple question I can get a better understanding of the situation and set myself up for success.

As for the monthly installment, I have multiple plans that would change the monthly payment without changing the price, and I would never open with the smallest one. If I did that, and the monthly installments were out of their comfort zone, then the only way I would be able to lower it would be to lower the price, and consequently cut into my commission. So, start with the shortest payment plan you have and extend it as necessary to find a monthly installment that the homeowner is comfortable with.

If they were stuck on the overall price of the project, then I would attempt to drop work or offer a less expensive product option. This gives me a chance to still write up an order and not diminish my commission as a percent. Although my commission will be smaller than the larger sale, I will still get a larger percentage of the sale as my commission than if I merely lowered the price on the same amount of work. You never know, the customer may feel that something of lower quality and or price may be the right solution for them. Instead of doing the same work for a lower price, do less work for a lower price. This keeps you extremely honest and credible and allows you to check your customer's temperature on the project.

IN HOME SALES

Let me provide an example of dropping work and not price. This involves a house that has a detached garage. I would say:

"Mr. and Mrs. Jones, instead of doing the house and the garage why don't we start with just the home? I know you would like to get it all done now, but how do you eat an elephant? One bite at a time. Let's start with the home. While the garage is important; no one lives in the garage. The family lives here and the roof has some substantial damage. We all know the longer it goes the more wood will have to be replaced and the more expensive the solution will be. We do not want any more moisture to get into the attic and develop into toxic mold or anything like that. Let's be smart and take care of the roof on the main house. Instead of spending $28,351, it will be $23,655. That comes out to be approximately $90 to $125 less a month. Let's get this done, and then in a year or two when you are ready to do the garage, we will come back and take care of you as a VIP customer. Can we go ahead and earn your business today?"

Then I would stick my hand out for a handshake.

Switching the product or service to one of lesser cost or dropping work also sets you up for a very powerful close down the road, called a "bear trap." Quickly described, like a bear trap in the woods, it's camouflaged, it cannot be seen. Here's an example: If you were pitching a home that has a detached garage and the price to reroof the entire project was $28,351, you may offer to do just the house without the garage for $23,655, as described above. The homeowner thinks about it, but after some contemplation, they decide they'd rather get it all done at once. The bear trap in the scenario would be as follows: "Look Mr. And Mrs. Jones, I don't know if I can, but if I were able to do the roof on the house and the garage for just the price of the house–$23,655–would I be able to earn your business today?" (Stick out a firm handshake and smile)

If they say yes, you would solidify their commitment and then call your supervisor to justify the price drop. You can never drop the price of a project without the assistance of someone outside of your situation. That part is important because, if you can drop the price without getting any authorization, the homeowners is going to wonder why you didn't give them the lower price to begin with.

Although I'm describing the bear trap to you here, we would not use it quite yet in the process. We would save it for later in our closing. But you can see how it is related to the concept of dropping work.

After offering to drop work or change payment plans, some homeowners will stick to their objection and reject your offer. DON'T PANIC! As always, the response is to stay cool, calm, and collected and say, "No problem. Before I hit the bricks, to make sure I did my job to the best of my ability let me ask you ..." Then hit the following topics:

1. Company
- Is XYZ company a company you feel comfortable doing business with?
- What stood out to you guys the most?
- So we are the company for you?

2. Material
- Is the XYZ material what you want to see in your home?
- What did you like most about it?
- So, safe to say this is what you want in your home?

3. Warranty
- Is the warranty long enough?
- Is there anything you would like to add or remove from the warranty?
- Would you agree the best warranty is the one you don't have to use?
- Is this a warranty that gives you peace of mind?

4. Myself
- Do you think I was able to educate you on the condition of your home and your options?
- Do you feel I can make the project come to fruition for you?

I would then say, "Fantastic thank you so much for your time and hospitality. It sounds like you like the company, you love the material and warranty, and I check out as well. Could it be that you just wish this was a little bit more affordable?" Do not wait for them to answer, simply keep moving forward. "Look I totally understand, there may be a way I can help. No promises, let's not break out the pom poms just yet."

Marketing Home

Then I would explain an option for lowering the price:

"At XYZ company, we spend a ton of money on marketing. We do events, home shows, radio advertisements, direct mailers, door knockers, and more. At the end of each year, the owners review all the marketing and see what was the best return on investment, or ROI, for the company. You know year after year the simplest, most old-school form of marketing turns out to be the most beneficial to the company. You know what that is? Yard signs. See what we do, we

invest in your home, and we help you pay for the project with some of our marketing dollars. Do you know why? Because your neighbors are nosy. They check out work going on in their neighborhood every day as they're driving by or walking their dog. With yard signs, at the end of the job we end up with eight to twelve new clients.

So typically, when we do a marketing home, this is what the company asks for. They want you to put a sign in your yard, for 30-90 days. It's just a small sign with our information on it. Then they are going to ask permission to take before and after photos of your project, just like the ones I showed you earlier of my other clients. I would love to add your home to my portfolio. Depending on how they come out, they may be used on our website, mailers, or other forms of marketing for us. Then we ask for you to give us a written or video testimonial. You will not be scripted on what to say, we want you to share your honest experience of working with us from start to finish. They also ask you for 3 referrals. Now these are not people that have to purchase anything from us, just three people you think could take advantage of our services and are willing to hear us out.

And lastly, the most important part is price confidentiality. Like I said we are going to help pay for this project and take a hit on the chin. The goal of that is to have your home be a showcase home in the area and get another

10-12 jobs. So, if any of your neighbors ask you what you paid, mum's the word.

Now I know how my manager handles this, so on a job such as yours if we were able to get you approved for a marketing home, the cost would range between $23,321 and $27,651. If I can get somewhere in this range, can I earn your business today?" (Stick out a firm hand for a handshake).

If They Say YES

If we get a "yes," we are going to agree on a specific number before moving forward. So, I would ask them, "Where in this range do I have to be to earn your business today?" Of course, they usually give the smallest number. So, I will stick out my hand and say, "Of course; 23,321 up to what?" By saying this, the homeowner will usually spit out a higher number, adding some money back into the deal. Whatever number they say, I'm going to get a firm handshake and agree on that range. "So, anywhere between 23,321 and 26,000 we're a go?"

Following agreement on that range, I would say, "Fantastic let me get your credit card for the deposit and let me get my boss on the horn for approval." Do not slow things down at that point. You must keep the momentum rolling forward and solidify the deal. Once they give you the credit card for the deposit and shake your hand, you have to call your manager and ask for a marketing home. Describe the transformation of the home over the phone and explain how using it will benefit the company.

For example, you got to your appointment a little early and had an opportunity to scope out the neighborhood. There is tons of remodeling going on, and you saw a bunch of different homes that would benefit from using your company's services. You have to remember that your company is a business. Why would your boss want to give them a discount? Because it makes business sense and will help the company obtain more clients.

Once you justify the price drop with your manager, keep the momentum going. "Congratulations this is amazing! Go grab your driver's license, I'll get the paperwork started."

If They Say NO

First, it is crucial to recognize that when homeowners present objections at this stage, what they're often indirectly communicating is a desire for a better price. Direct negotiation is not a typical aspect of American culture, so homeowners tend to express their concerns through more general objections rather than explicitly stating their wish for a better price. We want to continue negotiating without it appearing as a negotiation.

If the homeowner says "no" when you ask them about the marketing program, simply say, "No problem. You do agree that the marketing home price is more attractive than our regular MSRP? You surely will not call me back to do business at that price down the road, right? So, let me try and lock you in on this marketing home program for if and when you guys decide to move forward." I would immediately take my phone out and call my manager for a "future" marketing home.

This call to your manager starts exactly like the one described above, but instead of asking for a marketing home, you are asking to get the homeowner approved for a "FUTURE" marketing home. The key here is for your manager to know whether or not you have a commitment from the homeowner. So, when we have commitment we call for a marketing home, and when we do not have a commitment we call for a future marketing home. "Future" is the secret code word distinguishing between the two.

Since you do not have a commitment from the homeowner, you must exert a lot of pressure on the phone, really pushing to get it approved and explaining how amazing it will look when it is finished. One of the most important parts to understand here is that the homeowner is not currently moving forward, and as much as you may want to tell them how badly they need the service and remind them of the damage on their home, it would not behoove you to do so.

IN HOME SALES

Instead, we tell our manager all of this and let the homeowners overhear it. We are really talking to the homeowner through our conversation with the manager.

Despite all your efforts, your manager is going to deny your request and tell you there is no budget left for marketing in that zip code. You will then fight for the homeowners and ask if they can get funds from a neighboring zip code. Still, your manager will deny your request. "What about some extra manufacturer's credits." Again, the response will be "no."

Unlike many other closing techniques where it is the salesman versus the homeowner, this technique allows you to side with the homeowner and assist them in making this project come to fruition. Instead of you against them, it is you and them against the company. You have become the third owner of the property and will do anything to help the owners, including taking their side against your company.

From here, the manager will guide you and ask, "Why are you pushing for this so much? Is it the homeowner or the neighborhood?"

Your response will be "both." The homeowners are super nice, but you understand that this is a business, and this home would be a beacon for the company in a neighborhood buzzing with renovation potential.

Using the same reasoning as you would if the homeowners had agreed to the marketing program, you would explain to the manager, "I got here a little early and drove around, and there are a ton of homes that need work. One across the street needs paint, and other neighbors need a roof. I promise I can get you eight to ten jobs in this area alone. I will even come knock on doors on Sunday if necessary."

The manager would then ask if you are still in front of the homeowner, and the response would be affirmative. Then a conversation could go as follows:

Manager: "Wow this is not the right way to go about this. This is very unprofessional. Wouldn't it make more sense to follow up with the homeowner and come see me in the office, rather than put us both on the spot? I understand you are trying to help, but there are more appropriate ways to do this. Look this is what I'll do, I'll piggyback you onto Ryan's commercial job he's doing out in Temecula. Have you explained all of the marketing to them? Are they ok with all the stipulations? OK, do not put anything in the computer like you normally would. Instead, come into the office first thing tomorrow and hand this directly to me. I'll authorize it. Make sure you write in the addendum that the customer still gets the residential warranty. Also, you're going to have to go knocking on doors yourself and get me at least 7-10 new homes in the area, so I can justify this to my supervisor."

Rep: "Since we are putting this on a commercial order, does that mean that I can give them the commercial pricing?"

IN HOME SALES

Manager: "Are you serious? Are you really asking me in front of the homeowner? Give it to them this once and please give me a call as soon as you are out of there."

At that point you can, again, address the homeowners directly. "Well, looks like my loss is your gain. Don't worry about him, I will get them a lot of work and make up for this. He will be ok. You guys are so lucky. Commercial pricing is even better than the marketing homes deal. You are now getting this job basically at cost! CONGRATULATIONS for getting the best deal ever! Go grab your driver's license, I'll get the paperwork started." Then start filling out the paperwork.

When you get to this stage, many times the homeowner will just act accordingly and give you their driver's license out of the excitement of getting a better deal. Remember this is all they really wanted, and they feel unique and special knowing that they are getting something they are not supposed to get. However, there are times when the homeowner will stop and ask, "So how much is it?" This is when you will show them a price that is a little bit lower than the lowest price they have already seen. Recall that in my example we offered a price between $23,321 and $27,651 and they said "no." So we need to give them a number lower than 23,321. And it is critical that you know your numbers—the top, middle, and bottom that your company will allow you to sell the job for.

By this point, you should have the yes and be moving forward with an order. On the rare chance that you've given the commercial price and they are still saying no, but haven't asked you to leave, it means you're still in the pocket. This is where we begin what I call the romance of the sale. It's time to drop our own guards and come from a frame of curiosity. When a salesperson fails to close with someone who needs what they offer, it's often because they didn't discover everything about the client's situation to properly close the deal. In other words, we didn't ask enough prying questions. Now is the time to dig deeper.

Ask them, "You've agreed that you need a roof, and I have the roof you want done by a company you feel comfortable with. Help me understand what's stopping us from moving forward today?" When said in a soft, curious tone, this question opens the conversation to become more personal and transparent. At this point, if framed correctly, the buyer will reveal their true objection.

I've always said, "Half my job is educating you and presenting our offering, and the other half is helping you figure out how to get it done." This mindset creates an atmosphere of trust, making the buyer feel comfortable enough to fully express their reservations. Once these concerns are uncovered, they're typically easy to address. As discussed earlier, this could mean a smaller deposit, delaying the job by a couple of weeks until the money comes in, or removing the progress payment. Hence, they only pay a deposit and completion.

For example, if it's uncovered that they're waiting for a bonus from work expected in four weeks and won't have the money for the progress payment until then, you now understand their timeline. You can confirm that the deposit is okay and explain that you can delay the project start for three weeks, remove the progress payment, and by the time the project is done in four weeks, they can pay the completion. You'd be amazed how often timeline is the real issue, and buyers refuse to disclose it. If you do not want to delay the job start, you can also simply put them on a short no-interest, no-payment loan as well.

By being curious and asking the tough questions, you can get to the real meat and potatoes to help them make the decision. Remember, you want them to buy from you, not feel like they were sold. There's a big difference in that mindset. If you're able to master the art of romance and curiosity during the close, you'll find yourself not just making sales, but building lasting relationships with satisfied customers.

This approach may seem untraditional, and some might even view it as scammy or akin to a car salesman's tactics. However, it's essential to remember the psychology behind selling and buying. Homeowners often object to committing immediately because they believe it's the responsible thing to do. Many have been raised with the idea that they should get three bids and shop around. Why? Because they want to ensure they're getting the best deal possible and not overpaying. Although most people will never explicitly state this, it's a common undercurrent in these sales calls. Think about your own experiences shopping for cars: do you accept the first price the salesperson offers? Do you agree to the first monthly payment option presented? More often than not, you push back, trying to secure a better deal.

So, when you are sitting at the kitchen table, the homeowner is going through the same process. Although some reps are uncomfortable making these calls, this is the only way to make the homeowner feel unique and special. People jump on the deal because they feel they are getting something they are not supposed to get. Closing on the first visit is about making the homeowner feel they are winning. The truth is, they are, as long as your company does an incredible job performing the work or service you have described in your presentation.

Let's back up and go a little more in-depth into the drop sequence and the psychology behind it, along with why I feel this is not a shady business tactic. First and foremost, the marketing home is one of the oldest and truest ways of growing a business. Before search engine optimization, pay-per-click, and all these fancy forms of advertising, how did people do business? The combination of word-of-mouth and referrals is the oldest and truest way to grow a supportive following.

Similar to word-of-mouth and referrals is putting a yard sign out front. There is no secret that neighbors are snoopy, some more than others. When you drive down your street and see someone's roof being torn off, you rubber neck and look. When you come back home, you look over and see what kind of progress the crew made that day. The next day you look again. Humans are naturally wired to be curious. So, if companies spend tons of money on advertising, such as billboards, direct mailers, radio, and TV spots, why wouldn't it make sense to invest some money into a project where they can do live advertising and grow their customer base?

Neighbors also want to keep up with the Joneses. They see the roof being done, or the windows being installed, or whatever service it may be, and automatically start thinking about their own home: When was the last time our roof was done? How old are our windows? When was the last time we had a pest control service done?

This is the natural mindset of human beings. Although we know we shouldn't be comparing ourselves to others, we inevitably do. So, in this line of business, why wouldn't I invest a few thousand dollars to acquire a new client and then have the potential to acquire a dozen more? It is pretty standard for our reps to get a minimum of two to three jobs on the same street every time we do this.

Slapping our yard signs in front of a dozen homes in the same neighborhood is not just a good strategy; it's pure gold. Imagine cruising down the street and your name pops up on every other lawn. It sparks curiosity. "Who's this company making waves?" "If everyone's choosing them, they have to be top-notch, right?" It nudges folks to think, "Hey, maybe it's time we give them a shout."

The marketing home concept isn't about haphazardly cutting deals; it's about smart investment. Think of it as turning a satisfied customer's home into a live showcase—a real-deal advertisement that speaks louder than any billboard could. For the homeowner, it's a ticket to extra savings. For us, it's like laying down roots in the neighborhood and setting up a beacon that screams quality and trust. Every yard sign and every happy customer is a shout-out to potential clients, a way to spread the word without spending a dime on flashy ads. It's about making connections, one lawn at a time.

When a homeowner initially declines the marketing home offer because he is hesitant or unable to commit, transitioning to a "future" marketing home, and offering the commercial price drop, addresses their concerns about affordability without sacrificing the quality or scope of work. It shows our flexibility and commitment to meeting their needs, reinforcing their trust in our company.

The psychology behind it, again, is they are getting something they are not supposed to be getting. You called the manager to lock them in on the marketing home price for the future and all of a sudden, the call leads to an even bigger savings, one they normally would not be able to get. Of course, there are some embellishments and acting involved, as you end up putting yourself in an awkward position with your manager, even getting in a bit of trouble. This is part of the show. The customer feels sympathy for you and is ecstatic about the extra savings he is not supposed to be getting. Once you present this lower price to them, it's almost as if moving forward with you is a no-brainer.

    Although to some it may seem a little pushy, once a homeowner gets the better deal, they are usually ecstatic at the opportunity to get the work done at a more affordable price. It is also amazing to see how quickly the objections disappear. They are either more comfortable with the new price or believe that they are getting something they are not supposed to be getting, so they feel the urgency to jump on the deal of a lifetime.

    Sam Taggart in the "ABC of Closing," talks about how closing is honorable. He says, "Don't be ashamed of pushing someone into a decision." He then goes on to say "Believe in what you're selling, much more than the customer will ever initially believe in it. They will naturally push back on what you're selling, but you need to see past that and imagine three months or three years down the road when that service (or product) is making a significant difference in their lives." He then goes on to talk about the pride you should have as a closer.

He could not be more right! I have never gone back to a customer that I have closed to find that they were disappointed with their decision to move forward. On the contrary, they are always thanking me for giving them the extra push that they needed to make the decision. Often, they say, "We have been wanting to do this for years, and we are so grateful you gave us that extra push to get it done." The reps I have trained say the same thing, and they find that visiting these customers and seeing how thrilled they are with the result of the work is one of the most rewarding parts of the job.

IN HOME SALES

Chapter 17

Post-Close

Once the sale is made it is vital to post-close the sale. Equally as vital as a compelling warm-up is a solid cool-down. Racing out the door with signed work orders and a deposit in hand might risk leaving a sour taste with the homeowner. Thus, it's vital to spend a few extra moments to transition smoothly from the excitement of closing to affirming their decision. Reiterate the work order details, tidy up your samples, and then shift gears slightly.

I will tell my new customer, "I know we have had a lot of fun here today and everyone is excited to get the work done, but I have to get serious with you for a moment. One of my goals every day is to improve at my job, so would you mind sharing with me why I was able to earn your business today?" If your company leaves a folder or any paperwork behind, I would write down their reasons on the inside of the folder. The homeowner is solidifying why they chose to move forward with you.

After they share their reasons with you, I would then tell them, "I have an amazing reputation at my office. Not only do my coworkers and managers love me, but my customers do as well. So, I have to ask you. Is there any reason you may wake up in the middle of the night and get cold feet? Because if you are at all hesitant on moving forward with me, I would rather us not do this and part as friends."

Once they tell me that they are 100% ready to move forward, I will then ask them in a very nonchalant way, "who is the first person you're going to tell the good news to? What will they say?" The point of this line of questioning is to find out if there is anyone who may wizard my sale. The wizard is a third party who was not involved and who will suggest that they cancel the deal. If I can get some intel on this, it helps me to coach them on what to say back to this individual to protect my sale. Once I do this, and everything seems solid, I will change the subject and simply enjoy their company. The harder you had to close, the longer you need to stay and cool down the sale.

Chapter 18

Taking Care of Your Clients

To truly excel in this industry and tap into the potential for significant earnings, it's imperative to view every lead not as a one-off sale but as the beginning of an ongoing relationship. The real secret to making BIG money lies in nurturing each lead as if it were your last, recognizing that the close of a sale marks the start of a new opportunity. Too often, sales reps pour their efforts into securing a deal, only to move on swiftly afterward, leaving behind a wealth of untapped potential. What many fail to realize is that the homeowner's journey with your products and services is just beginning. Visit your customers throughout the job. Do not abandon them after you get their deposit check and signed work order.

I have always recommended to my reps to take the time to write a handwritten thank you card to all their customers. Write it the day you close and make sure it hits the mail the next day. If you're going to be in the area the next day on other appointments, stop by and drop it off. A small gift also goes a long way with the customer. If there is something that you discussed with them, that you know they will like, get them that. If not, a box of cookies, flowers, or a bottle of wine are all great options. The price of the gift is not important. What is important is that you took the time to stop by and thank them again for the opportunity to serve them. This is also a phenomenal post-close and ensures your customer does not get cold feet and back out of the deal.

You have already invested hours building trust during the initial appointment, laying the groundwork for a lasting relationship. This is your opportunity to capitalize on that trust. We are not just any company; we are a great company offering top-notch products and services that homeowners dream of. It's essential to understand that the desire for a beautiful home never truly ends for a homeowner. Once they embark on one project, they are often eager to continue improving their space until it meets their every aspiration.

By presenting your clients with enticing deals post-sale, you're not just earning commissions; you're essentially collecting on the trust and rapport you've already established—consider it "free money." Remember, if you don't seize this opportunity, rest assured that someone else will. Your clients don't just want to make a single purchase; they're looking to transform their homes over time, and they need a trusted advisor to guide them through this journey. You were the one that initially put them in the home improvement state of mind, you might as well be the one to help them continue.

This approach of treating each lead as the beginning of a long-term relationship, rather than the end of a sales transaction, is what sets apart the truly successful in our field. It's about continuous engagement, ensuring satisfaction, and being available as a resource for the next project and the next.

Moreover, revisiting the client during the project not only allows for the opportunity to upsell or introduce additional services, but also lays the groundwork for generating referrals. Demonstrating ongoing interest and care in the client's project significantly increases the likelihood that they will recommend you to their friends, family, and coworkers. This is also a prime time to go knock on the neighbors' doors and introduce yourself. I have found that a simple apology for any inconvenience caused by noise or dust that the crew might be making is a great way to start a conversation, whether it is truly necessary or not.

People will be much more receptive to talking to you if you start the conversation out this way rather than with a sales pitch. Then you can go on to discuss the work you're doing at their neighbor's home and offer to provide a free quote for any home improvement that you see they may need. By knocking on every door within eyesight of the current project, you not only expand your reach, but you also solidify your presence in the community, often leading to additional jobs through just being visible and proactive.

Utilizing these strategies transforms every project into not just a job, but a steppingstone toward assembling a more extensive network of satisfied customers and potential leads. It's about more than just sales; it's about building a community around your brand and services, proving that genuine care and strategic engagement can pave the way to success in the home improvement industry.

Chapter 19

Tips for Success

Role play:

This is the most effective yet least used exercise out there. Reps either feel they are too good for it or are too embarrassed to role-play in front of their colleagues. Regardless of their excuse, this is crucial to mastering the art of one-call close sales. It is essential to "practice how you play." If you fail to practice and engrain this material in your head, and most importantly on your tongue because this is a speaking job, you will continue to be mediocre and will find your goals much harder to achieve.

When you do roleplay, it is essential to do so with your co-workers and managers, and not your spouse, boyfriend, or girlfriend. The latter love you, think you are amazing, and will fail to tell you where you are messing up. Also, they have not attended the training that you have, and they simply don't know what they don't know. Your co-workers and managers will know the script and will help ensure that you master not only the words, but also the body language, tone, speed, and voice inflection to make your message the most powerful one possible.

Write out your scripts:

Writing out sales scripts is an incredibly powerful tool for any sales rep aiming to excel in the home improvement industry. This practice engages multiple learning modalities, significantly enhancing the retention and mastery of sales techniques. When you write out your scripts, you're not just passively reading them; you're actively engaging with the material. Reading the script hones your understanding, saying it out loud reinforces your verbal delivery, and writing it down solidifies the information in your memory.

This triple reinforcement ensures that the script becomes second nature, allowing for more natural and effective communication with potential clients. This method of learning fosters a deeper internalization of sales strategies, ensuring that when the moment comes to engage with a customer, the words flow seamlessly and persuasively.

Let go of limiting beliefs:

Henry Ford said, "Whether you think you can, or you think you can't—you're right." It means you determine your own success or failure. If you think you can, you will succeed or somehow find a way to do it. So why not tell yourself, "I can" and make boatloads of cash? I constantly tell everyone I train, this job is 50% attitude, 25% knowledge, and 25% closing. Too often I hear reps say they need more product knowledge, better leads, or cheaper prices.

The truth is that what you need is a better attitude and a stronger belief in yourself. Oftentimes on the group sales chat, I will ask the reps to write, "I can close anyone, anywhere, anytime!" The purpose is to psych them up and spur them to start believing in themselves. Tyler Ward, one of the owners of Tidal Remodeling, even printed this on a shirt for the reps! Mindset is so important that you may even argue that it's 80% of the job.

Set goals, multiply them by ten, and charge forward:

Be a trailblazer in your industry. It doesn't matter what the average guy is doing or what the top guy is doing. If your goals are bigger and you believe in them with every ounce of your body, then go set new records and live the life of your dreams. If you are the top guy and want to grow, then find new people to surround yourself with. If they are not available to you in person, then use social media as a tool for growth and not as a tool for the consumption of nonsense. It has never been easier than it is in today's modern world to find inspiration on social media. I personally follow loads of people who inspire me to level up and think bigger.

Another way to get around people of high value is to attend seminars and masterminds and to join exclusive online forums and groups that focus on personal and professional development. These spaces are not just about networking; they're about immersing yourself in environments where growth, ambition, and success are the common languages spoken. Being part of such communities exposes you to new ideas, strategies, and mindsets that challenge you to push beyond your current boundaries. Remember, if you're the smartest person in the room, you're in the wrong room. By constantly seeking out those who are further along the path you wish to tread, you not only accelerate your learning curve but also open doors to opportunities you might not have imagined.

So, make it a mission to continuously seek out and engage with these high-caliber groups. Let their achievements and drive inspire you to set loftier goals and achieve greater success. Because, in the end, the path to extraordinary achievements is often paved with the wisdom and encouragement of those who've walked the journey before us.

This is precisely why I've put together the OCCA Facebook group and the OCCA Accelerator Summit. These platforms offer a golden opportunity to mingle with like-minded individuals, all hungry for growth and eager to share their experiences, strategies, and victories. These spaces are your launchpad for breaking the mold, setting new benchmarks, and carving out your path to exceptional achievements. It's where the dreamers gather, where visions are shared, and where the seeds of greatness are sown and nurtured.

IN HOME SALES

Conclusion

As I draw the curtains on the lessons, stories, and strategies shared, I find myself reflecting on the essence of what it means to master the art of the one-call close. It's not just about sales tactics, overcoming objections, or even closing deals on the spot. It's about a deeper understanding of human connection, the value we bring to every interaction, and the impact we leave on the lives we touch through our work. This book is not merely a guide to enhancing your sales skills; it's a testament to the power of belief, resilience, and the relentless pursuit of excellence. It's about transforming ordinary opportunities into extraordinary achievements, not just for the sake of sales, but for the fulfillment of helping others achieve their dreams of a better home.

As you move forward, armed with the knowledge and insights shared within these pages, remember that success in one-call close—or in any aspect of life—begins with the courage to take the first step, the conviction to push through challenges, and the vision to see beyond the immediate transaction. It's about building relationships, not just making sales; about becoming a trusted advisor, not just a salesperson; and about leaving a legacy of integrity and excellence.

IN HOME SALES

So, as you close this book, don't see it as the end of your learning journey but as the beginning of a new chapter in your professional life. Take the lessons learned, the strategies developed, and the stories shared, and use them to fuel your passion for greatness in everything you do. The path to mastery is a continuous journey, full of challenges, learning, and growth. Embrace it with an open heart and a determined spirit.

Remember, the world of one-call close is not just about transactions; it's about transformations—transforming spaces, lives, and ultimately, yourself. As you go forth, carry with you the belief in your ability to make a difference, the commitment to your personal and professional growth, and the relentless pursuit of excellence in every call, every close, and every life you touch.

This is not the end but a new beginning—a call to action to rise above the ordinary, to push the boundaries of what's possible, and to achieve the extraordinary. With every call, every close, and every challenge, you have the opportunity to leave an indelible mark on the world. Seize it with both hands, embrace the journey, and let's make every call count.

Here's to your success, to the lives you'll transform, and to the legacy you'll build, one-call close at a time.

Join Our Journey Beyond the Pages

As we close this chapter together, I want to remind you that our journey doesn't end here. The path to mastering the art of the one-call close is ongoing, and I'm committed to walking it alongside you, providing support, inspiration, and a community where we can all grow together.

I encourage you to connect with me further and dive deeper into the world of transformational sales techniques and strategies. Here's how you can stay engaged, get more resources, and become a part of a like-minded community dedicated to excelling in the home improvement industry:

- **Social Media Connections**: Follow me on Instagram @ShaiAdes, where I share daily insights, tips, and personal anecdotes. My goal is to inspire, motivate, and challenge you to reach new heights in your sales career.
- **One Call Close Academy Facebook Group**: This vibrant community is your go-to place for collaboration, sharing best practices, and learning from fellow sales professionals committed to the art of the one-call close. Join us at https://www.facebook.com/groups/onecallcloseacadem

y/ and start engaging with peers who are just as passionate about sales excellence as you are.

- **OCCA Vault**: Unlock a treasure trove of knowledge with the OCCA Vault, your premium access to an extensive library of video training sessions designed to sharpen your skills, refine your strategies, and boost your sales performance. Dive into the vault here: Onecallcloseacademy.com and begin exploring the comprehensive resources tailored for your success.
- **OCCA Accelerator Summit**: Don't miss this immersive experience designed to catapult your sales career to unprecedented levels. The Accelerator Summit is a convergence of the best minds in the business, offering workshops, networking opportunities, and insights from industry leaders. Secure your spot at the next summit, Onecallcloseacademy.com and prepare for a transformative journey.
- **OCCA Sales Tool Box**: As a token of my appreciation for your commitment to growth, I'm offering a free download of the "OCCA Sales Tool Box: Your Ultimate Sales Strategy Kit for Home Improvement Success." This eBook is packed with practical tools, checklists, and strategies to streamline your sales process and maximize your one-call close rate. Download your free copy here: Onecallcloseacademy.com and start leveraging these invaluable resources today.

SHAI ADES

The journey to sales mastery is not one to be walked alone. It's a path paved with challenges, learning, and triumphs. By connecting with me through these platforms, you're not just gaining access to resources; you're becoming part of a community committed to excellence, growth, and mutual success.

I look forward to continuing our journey together, pushing boundaries, and achieving new milestones. Let's turn the page to the next chapter of our adventure, where your growth is limitless, and the possibilities are endless.

Thank you for being part of this journey. Here's to our continued success, together.

Made in the USA
Coppell, TX
06 February 2026